Topsy Turvy
in
The Church of the Nazarene

Wayne G. Greve

Copyright © 2010 by Wayne G. Greve

Topsy Turvy in The Church of the Nazarene
by Wayne G. Greve

Printed in the United States of America

ISBN 9781612150161

All rights reserved solely by the author. The author guarantees all contents are original and do not infringe upon the legal rights of any other person or work. No part of this book may be reproduced in any form without the permission of the author. The views expressed in this book are not necessarily those of the publisher.

Unless otherwise indicated, Bible quotations are taken from The Holy Bible In Its Original Order. Copyright © 2007 by York Publishing Company. Used by Permission; and The King James Version.

Some names, initials, and places have been changed to protect the innocent.

www.xulonpress.com

Dedication

To my wife Marilyn and son Rodney who have stood unflinchingly by my side. To all who have been wounded by the conduct of others in the Visible Church on earth, may you find healing. Lastly, to the Church growth experts everywhere.

Heartfelt thanks to:

- Martha Byerly for unstinting efforts in the computer work which went into the production of this book.
- To Philip Skarich, who designed the cover of this book.
- To the bruised minority who shared their pain and insights.

Introduction

In part, this book reflects a personal Auto-biography. This includes wearing two hats for many years.

In some ways this story is an expose of the inner workings of a Church. To some this may be scandalous but honesty depicts that it needs to be told. Eph.5: 11 says ". . . and have no fellowship with the unfruitful works of darkness, but expose them." It seems imperative that other innocent people need to know what goes on behind the scenes.

The research the author has done with respect to two Nazarene Districts has been hard won. The author's eyeballs have burned pouring over fine print journals and statistics that are not too reliable. Many times he had to resort to the use of a magnifying glass. The author trusts that the appendices will give church leaders food for thought. Church growth experts should be interested in what he has to share.

Lastly, the author has no visible "great names" to endorse this book. He is a voice crying from the "Sidewalk Jungles" of America for the helpless minority and others who may land in similar circumstances. The author believes that there is a church within the visible Church which is the bride of Christ. As Christians, the author and his wife continue to put their trust in the sustaining power of a graceful and loving God.

Yes, in some places, the author is preaching to the Choir!

Acronyms Used in This Book

DS – District Superintendent
DAB – District Advisory Board
HT – Holiness Today
DNR – Department of Natural Resources
WMA – World Mission Areas
CTM – Church Type Mission

Book Organization
TOPSY TURVY

In the
CHURCH OF THE NAZARENE

Chapter One	Birth of the Church of the Nazarene	15
Chapter Two	Clintonville, 1972	20
Chapter Three	Sale of Clintonville	28
Chapter Four	802 Days	34
Chapter Five	Development of Christ Community	38
Chapter Six	Years Following Christ Community, 1985-1999	62
Chapter Seven	First Years at Indianapolis First Church, 1999-2002	74
Chapter Eight	Christ Community Becomes Crossroads, 2002	79
Chapter Nine	First Church from 2002-2008	83

Chapter Ten	The Prince Arrives, 2008 (September)	90
Chapter Eleven	Ironclad Power, 2009	120
Chapter Twelve	Crossroads Collapses, 2009 7-29-2009 (7 years) history	132
Chapter Thirteen	Topsy Turvy	136
Chapter Fourteen	What's Ahead Bible number associated with deliverance or salvation	152
Appendices		159

"In the beginning . . ." Gen. 1:1

Chapter One

Birth of the Church of the Nazarene – A Time Line

I. Before the Church of the Nazarene

The Mayflower
1718 Yale College
1730 – 40s Birth of Methodism
1735 Moravians
1737 John Wesley
1739 Whitefield - First Awakening
1741 Jonathon Edwards
1756 Princeton
1764 Brown University
1765 Stamp Act
1766 Queen's College
1769 Dartmouth
1770 Jefferson
1775 Daniel Boone, Paul Revere and John Wesley
1775 American Revolution
1776 Declaration of Independence
1777 Our Flag
1779 Freedom of Religion
1782 British Surrender

1784 American Methodists Emerge
1790 Second Great Awakening
1792 First Methodist Conference
1801 Cane Ridge, Kentucky
1830 Methodists Change
1834 Camp Meetings and Circuit Riders
* ⎰ 1838 Phineas Bresee Born
    1843 Wesleyan Methodist Church
    1844 - 45 Methodists Split
    1860 Free Methodists
    1861 Civil War
    1871 Moody
    1880 – 90 Holiness Movement
    1890 – 94 Crises
    1895 Church of the Nazarene organized first Sunday in October

*Contemporary with Dr. Bresee

The Nazarenes Emerge

1838 Bresee Born
1856 Conversion
1857 - 58 Marengo
1858 Pella
1860 Back to New York and Marriage
1860 Grinell
    Galesburg
1862 Des Moines Circuit
    Appointed presiding Elder Winterset
1866 Centennial of Methodism
1866 Fall – appointed to Chariton
1866 Sanctified
1870 Appointed to Council Bluffs
1871 Elected to General Conference
1873 Red Oak
1876 Clarinda

1879 Creston
1881 Back to Council Bluffs
1881- 83 Goes into business
1886 Appointed to First Methodist Pasadena
1891 Asbury Methodist L.A. District
1891 Presiding Elder L.A. District
1892 Removed from presiding Elder – sent to Simpson
1893 Appointed to Boyle Heights
1894 Forced Out – Mission
1895 Church of the Nazarene founded
1896 Moving Again
1901 Rev C. W. Ruth, Indianapolis
1903 March to the new church [1]

Bresee was born in 1838 in New York State. The controversy between Methodists and what would be the Free Methodist Church was heating up. In 1860, it resulted in a group of people being expelled from the Genesee Conference of the Methodist Episcopal Church. This took place in western New York State. Ironically these people were accused of being Nazarites in a secret association.

Phineas Bresee would have been about 22 years old at the time that the birth of Free Methodism began. Genesee County is between Buffalo and Rochester, New York. Delaware County, where Phineas Bresee was born, is east of Genesee County and between Ithaca, New York and the Catskill Mountains. The two areas were only separated by three or four counties.

The men accused of being Nazarites included Roberts, Stiles, McCreery and others. Thirty five years later Bresee, now on the west coast, would found the Church of the Nazarene. I have never read this, but it is a theory of mine. All these men grew up in the Methodist Episcopal Church in roughly the same area.

I believe that when Bresee selected the name, Church of the Nazarene that he might have been partially influenced by the name attached to the dissidents in the Methodist Episcopal Church. This all happened in the area where he grew up. These people were called Nazarites and later they became Free Methodists.

Between 1830 -1870 the Methodists began to change. On the heels of this, what was known as the Moody – Sankey revival began to emerge between 1871 – 1891. This revival took place in large cities in America and Britain. In a visit to London they had 285 meetings attended by two million five hundred and thirty thousand people.

In the same time frame the Sunday School emerged as a great interdenominational movement. "Jacobs, a Baptist and Vincent, a Methodist, influenced the Fifth National Sunday School Convention, to adopt uniform Sunday-School Lessons."[2]

Between 1880 and 1900 more splits began to occur out of the Methodist Church. Complaints emerged that the church was becoming too formal and that she was leaving her first love. So called, "heart religion" was disappearing. The Wesleyan doctrine of entire sanctification was being changed.

Groups emphasizing the doctrine of holiness were emerging in the North, the South, the East and the West. These groups taught Justification, Cleansing, and Baptism of the Spirit. Some believed in the premillennial return of the Lord, speaking in tongues and divine healing.[3]

Between 1890 – 1894 the people who believed in Holiness reached a crisis. They began to break off from mainline churches. More than 25 different bodies were organized. The Church of the Nazarene was the largest. It was formed in 1895. It adopted a policy of ingesting other groups of like mindedness through the process of mergers.

Others that came on the American scene were:

The Church of God
Christian Missionary Alliance
General Council of the Assemblies of God
Volunteers of America
American Rescue Workers
Reformed Methodist Church
Wesleyan Methodist Church (1843, earlier)
Free Methodist Church (1860, earlier)
Pilgrim Holiness Church (1922, later)

Representatives of these people were men like Asa Maham, Dwight Moody, R.A. Torrey, Charles Finney and Thomas Upham. Also, there were others like Phineas Bresee and B. T. Roberts to name a few. The largest membership and leadership came out of the Methodists.[4]

Some were expelled from their churches. Others like Phineas Bresee were forced out, but one way or another they came out and were sometimes referred to as "Come Outers."

Phineas Bresee was forced out of his church on the third Sunday of October, 1895. He describes his feelings like this. "I scarcely knew any other home relationship in the church than the annual conference, and when I laid it down everything pertaining to the church which I had so loved and labored for, my heart was full of almost unbearable sadness. The night was spent in much prayer, and with many tears." The church of the Nazarene was organized in a hall provided at 317 South Main Street, in Los Angeles, California. On the third Sunday of October 100 charter members were enrolled. The charter member list was kept open for a few days and consummated with 135 members.[5]

I don't know at what point my wife's family became Nazarenes, but I do know that her grandfather D. gave 50 years to the Nazarenes. I know that her father gave another 50 years and I know that we gave 50 years of available service. I know that our real service began at a place called Clintonville and there we will share part of our Journey.

"Now after he had patiently endured, he attained the promise."
Heb. 6:15

Chapter Two

Clintonville

This is a Nazarene story. Our involvement with the Church of the Nazarene covers three generations. Those three generations represent 150 years of service to the church in various capacities. With that in mind I tell my story and the story of a church.

Clintonville is a road in Oakland County in Michigan. The average reader has never heard of it. It is in the suburbs of Pontiac, Michigan. On this road was a Nazarene Church by the same name. Little did my wife and I realize how a road would impact our lives! I had done some work for the Nazarenes and was a licensed minister at the time. I was also an educator in the public schools of Michigan. One day the phone rang and it was Dr. J.M.W. of the Eastern Michigan District of the Church of the Nazarene. He asked me if I would be interested in pastoring the Clintonville Church of the Nazarene.

It seemed that the pastor, H.K., had run amuck with the district and with the denomination. He had tried to take the property away from the Nazarenes.

Pastor H.K. seemed to be a hard-working man. He had built the church by sheer will-power and determination. He had floated a bond program of $100,000 to finance the construction of the church. He was a very convincing man and had successfully sold all the bonds. However, he was apparently promised help from the denomination.

This help did not materialize and now he was angry and determined to take the property and establish an independent church. All of this began to consummate in 1972. I agreed to become pastor of the church.

Prior to this I had been interim pastor of both Grace Church of the Nazarene and Hillcrest Church of the Nazarene. In both cases the D. S. had appointed one of his sons-in-law to become the permanent pastors, of the latter two churches.

Now, the Nazarenes needed a bi-vocational pastor because the Rev. H.K. had found a legal way to hold on to the parsonage. At least it appeared that this situation would exist for a while. The Rev. H.K. also held the church Sunday School bus. Eventually, he found a way to keep the church bus.

I will never forget that first Sunday service. The church could seat about 250 people and we had 8 people in the service that day. The bond program was structured so that each payment would increase. When a bond came due, the holder would present it to the church for redemption.

We never got out from under that pressure until the program was paid off. The interest was 7% I believe. What a day it was when we paid off the last bond!

As the Rev. H.K. left the property, he took a number of items with him. Because a few of his members stayed with the church, I was able to ascertain what things were gone. I thought on this for awhile and finally decided to file an insurance claim. Little did I know what was to follow.

The insurance company promptly filed a theft claim with the Michigan State Police. One night, when I was driving home from the church, a state police cruiser with flashing lights pulled me over to the side of the road. The patrolman walked up and said, "Reverend I need you to come back to your church and meet the Rev. H.K." I went back to my church office and there, in front of the state policeman the Reverend H.K. agreed to make restitution. Subsequently, the stolen goods were returned to the church.

What followed was beyond my wildest imagination. The Rev. H.K. seemed to have a bunch of hoods who would do his every bidding. The church was broken into repeatedly. One Sunday morning

I brought my family to church only to discover an awesome sight. The pulpit, which was in the shape of a cross, had been torn down and laid flat on the platform. The Nazarene Church Manual lay in the center of the cross. The sanctuary was littered with hymn books, Sunday School literature and anything else that was loose! My wife and I spent the Sunday School hour cleaning up the mess.

In the days ahead we called the state police many times. One day a trooper looked at me and said, "Pastor, why don't you quit and get out of here?" I said, "But I am trying to do God's work!"

In advanced days there were innumerable crank calls on my phone. They began running drugs from a nearby house right across the church parking lot. We eventually were forced to install a chain link fence around the entire property!

At our first district assembly when I gave my report, we were given a standing ovation by the assembly. We determined more than ever that we would salvage the church.

It wasn't long until the Rev. H.K. built a new church only about two blocks from the location of Clintonville. Over the next few years we would see the Rev. H.K. take families and individuals from us almost as fast as we could get them. He had the blessing of at least one prominent attorney in Oakland County. He was clever!

In the meantime, we had to go to court to recover the parsonage. We won and recovered it. However, they trashed it when they left! We had to borrow $5,000 from the district to repair it for occupancy.

We began to echo the Rhyme of the Ancient Mariner by Coleridge. "Day after day we stuck, nor breath nor motion as idle as a painted ship upon a painted ocean."[6] Year after year was going by and we would make a little progress. God seemed to help us make the bond payments.

In 1976 a reporter from the Pontiac-Waterford Times interviewed me and this is what he wrote.

Two Hatted Minister Helps Rebuild Church

The Reverend Wayne Greve is a man who wears "two hats."

On weekdays he works as a special education teacher in the West Bloomfield public school system, but spends the rest of his time pastoring the Clintonville Church of the Nazarene in Waterford Township, in Oakland County, Michigan.

"The fact that I have these two jobs may raise some people's eyebrows," the Rev. Greve said, "But if you study the history of the church you find that the church and education have always gone hand in hand. The church was the first group to put an emphasis on educating lay people."

"You often read of priests in Congress, in the scientific community and in the medical profession. There is a lot of history to support the fact that many men wore two hats and wore them effectively."

The Rev. Greve whose teaching background includes time spent as a professor of education at Northwest Nazarene College in Idaho, has headed the 27 year old Clintonville Church since 1972. He took over the church at a troubled time in its history. A new church had just been built when the congregation abandoned the church.

Saying that he did not want to "open old wounds," the Rev. Greve would not elaborate on the disagreement which caused the congregation to leave the church just when the new structure was completed. But, he did point out that the present congregation is entirely new.

"I came here in 1972 to try to rebuild the church," he said. "The membership is now over 40. We are growing and gaining back our momentum."

Such is the generosity of this small congregation with a big heart, that the average per capita donation to the church over the past four years has been in the range of $521 to $720 the Rev, Greve said. "We were a '10 percent' church last year," he added. "That means that 10 percent of our church budget was channeled into missionary activities."

Located at 4453 Clintonville Road, near the Independence Township border, the church presently draws its members from within a 15 mile radius, which includes the communities of Clarkston, Pontiac and Waterford.

"People no longer patronize only churches close to them," offered the pastor. "They may drive by five churches to get to the church they really want."

Even with the relatively small size of the new congregation, the Rev. Greve said, it is still tough to build a sense of Community in a vast metropolitan region like the Detroit area.

That is one reason why the church holds its Wednesday night Bible study programs in the home of a different member of the congregation each week.

"We do this in the homes, so our outreach is in terms of fellowship," he said. "In a metropolitan area it is easy to become impersonal to the point where people are not being reached. But we have found this home Bible study to be an effective ministry."

The short study sessions are usually followed by a prayer and then refreshments and 'chit chat' among the folks in attendance.

The Rev. Greve tries to extend this community feeling by holding potluck dinners once a month after the 11:00 a.m. Sunday services. (Sunday School is at 10:00 a.m. and evening worship is at 6:00 o'clock).

"In keeping with the general Nazarene denomination we try to emphasize Monday nights as family nights," he said. "We try to help families have more communication with each other. We feel the family is the critical unit in society today."

The denomination is Wesleyan in nature, which means that Nazarenes adhere to the doctrines espoused by religious leader John Wesley.

"We believe in the doctrine of sanctification," the Rev. Greve said. "We believe in the second coming of Christ, the final judgment, the resurrection of the dead and the virgin birth of Christ. We believe that man is a free moral agent created by God."

Closely related to the idea that man has free will, is the Wesleyan belief in being "born again." That phrase, of course, has become quite popular in recent months due to president-elect Jimmy Carter, a Baptist, professing to be a "born again Christian."

What does it mean to a person when he becomes "born again?"

"In essence, his life-style goes through some sort of revolution," Pastor Greve remarked. "He then begins to identify with the life of Christ. He begins to imitate the lifestyle of the Lord as laid down in the Sermon on the Mount and many passages of the Bible."

"We believe that changed lives are the only hope of the world." He continued. "Christianity does offer a viable way of solving man's conflicts in the political arena and other human endeavors."

The Nazarenes consider the Bible to be the inspired word of God, and feel that "everything written there is adequate to meet the needs of 20th century just as it was second or third century man," the Rev. Greve said.

But the pastor is a teacher too, and he explained that the Nazarenes have many colleges throughout the United States, colleges which offer both religious and liberal arts education.

When it comes to matters of faith, the Rev. Greve clearly wears the hat of a minister.

Time moved along. Our secular jobs kept us from going crazy. The Rev. H.K. put weekly pressure on us. We were growing slightly but not in proportion to the blood, sweat and toil that we were putting into the church." I started seeking other ways to move the church forward. These events started sometime prior to Thanksgiving in 1978.

Beliefs, Pastor Wayne G. Greve

Events Around 1978

1. I asked the District Superintendent about the possibility of a merger. The answer was No!
2. Shortly after my request, Grace Church was merged with Metropolitan which had already merged with another church. This became a church with a co-pastor.
3. Sometime in November of 1978 we had an emergency meeting with the Advisory Board. We asked if fund raisers could help us. (The bond payments were steeper and steeper). The Advisory Board took no action for us, but it wasn't long until professional fund raisers were all over the district for another church.

Events in 1979

1. Just prior to 1979 I had a number of conversations with Dr. Hurn in Kansas City, relative to our church. These conversations stemmed from contacts we had with him at a church growth seminar held in our local church, and again at a Bi-vocational Pastor's Seminar held in Kansas City. I was trying to secure a home mission gift from some large church in the denomination.
2. Dr. Hurn referred us back to our local district and Superintendent W.
3. Dr. W. referred us to Flint Central which was one of the largest churches on the district. (My wife's father had pastored it and under his ministry the current building was built at that time.) Later, this building would burn down.
4. Rev. B., the pastor, promptly referred us back to the District Advisory Board and C.C. We also made a further request for 2 home mission couples to come and help us. We never got an answer from anyone. So much for mission, so much for brotherly love! In the meantime the district authorized us to put Clintonville up for sale. This was ongoing.
5. We had another emergency Advisory Board meeting which produced no answers.

And so, day after day we carried on. Some days were crazy, but we felt committed to carry on the work. Being of German stock my father had taught me much about patience and perseverance. My work in education acted as a balance to help keep me stabilized against the "crazies" in our church work. We labored on, day after day, and watched events develop in our church lives.

"There will not be a funeral – there will be a resurrection." WG

Chapter Three

Sale of Clintonville

The district had now authorized the sale of Clintonville. After going through 100 organizations we sold the property to a Pentecostal group. The sale was on a land contract with a down payment and the balance due on a balloon payment in 90 days.

Of course, the group wanted possession as soon as possible. This meant that we would have to move out almost immediately.

We had many small articles which did not go with the sale of the church. There were enough items that we could not do it alone. We put in a request to the district for Men and Missions to come and help us move. We were informed that they would be at Olivet College to help build bleachers for football. We hired people to help us move and a local realtor in Ortonville offered us storage. It appeared that football was more important than church planting.

We had no place to worship until the local funeral director offered us his funeral parlor. Our congregation went into a freefall – they did not like worshipping in a funeral home!

One night in desperation I called the presiding General Superintendent. I tracked him to a motel in Miami, Florida. I told him about our situation and informed him that I was afraid we were dying. In a gruff voice he said "Let her die" and hung up. I was determined that after all we had put into the church, it was not going to die!

On the strength of my reputation as an educator I went to a local bank and got a loan for $75,000 on my signature. There were no payments until the note was due. This loan was to get our new building started.

The next battle erupted when, with an attorney, we took an option on ten acres of land in Clarkston, Michigan. This land was strategically located on M-15. The first complaint came from Lake Louise Nazarene about 8 miles north of Clarkston. We were infringing on their territory.

The second event was the local zoning board. I made the mistake of publishing a plan that God gave me in the holy land. It would be done in stages. I had taken my idea or vision to Bob Chenowith, a Nazarene architect. He had done a beautiful job. The problem was that the whole thing looked too grandiose.

By now our story was well publicized in the Community. There was a Lutheran man on the zoning board and he was determined not to let us build on the ten acres. He said "there is already too much tax-free property in this township."

The local newspaper got involved and we were ridiculed in newspaper articles. I called the Advisory Board for help. They advised me to call the District Superintendent for help, but the District Superintendent was out of the country. More people were leaving my church. It was becoming a lonely battle! One day my attorney looked at me and said "Reverend, why don't you give up on the ten acre option. It's like putting good money after bad money." I said "I agree." So we gave it up. The irony of this whole scene is that today, two beautiful churches are setting in the vicinity of our ten acre option.

Dr. W. advised us to leave the funeral home and so we began to worship in our homes. This continued throughout 1979-80 until we arrived at our first stage new plant at Goodrich, Michigan.

By now I was ready to resign but the District Superintendent advised me not to resign and to seek property between Goodrich and Davison, Michigan on M-15. I located a beautiful piece of property on a hill north of Goodrich. I found out that it belonged to a local farmer. It was not being farmed. I sent a local realtor to see if the farmer would sell it to us. He would not work with any realtor. The next Sunday I informed my little congregation of the results. They said, "Pastor, why don't you go and talk to the farmer yourself." I called the District Superintendent to go look at the property with me and he told me to buy it if I could. I then approached the farmer, and he sold it to me on the spot!   I sent a victory telegram to the General Superintendent and I never received a response! Hopefully, once again we were on our way with God's help. Certainly not with our denominations help!

At Assembly, I appealed to the presiding General Superintendent not to let Assembly close without the name, "Christ Community" being approved for our Church. He referred me back to Dr. W. Dr. W. resigned and the Assembly closed. We had no name!

My church members wanted the name "Christ Community." We never knew why this was such a hang-up. At the same time we were building our church the "Herald of Holiness," the church's denominational periodical, had published a two page article about a Nazarene Church in Wisconsin. This church had a bi-vocational pastor. Just like me. They named their new church "Christ Community Church of the Nazarene." But we couldn't!

Later on the Advisory Board finally agreed to let us name our new Church "Christ Community."

As the days slipped by I became concerned about getting things going. We had the property and it was riding on my signature.

We had the new superintendent at our home for dinner. We showed him our property plans, hopes and dreams. We asked for approval to sell the land contract on the Clintonville property. He gave us verbal approval and promised to send a letter of approval.

No letter of approval came and I continued to negotiate with a major company to buy the land contract.

Finally, I called the D.S. and asked why I had never received the letter of approval to market the land contract. I was informed that he had received bad vibrations from the Advisory Board about selling the land contract.

Also, when the District Superintendent was at our home for dinner, I had asked him to disorganize the Clintonville Church, because the new church would be in a community far removed from Clintonville. It would not even be in the same County! I never heard of any action to disorganize Clintonville at its obvious death. When we finally received approval for the name "Christ Community Church of the Nazarene," we just went ahead and incorporated the new name.

A few days later, I received a letter from Dr. G. telling me that the district wished to cut off all or part of my housing allowance. I suggested to him that this was about one week's notice. While this was going on, a rumor surfaced from the district office that we were bilking the district out of money. At this point 7 years of our lives had gone into trying to solve a Nazarene problem.

The district Advisory Board met in October and I received no housing allowance. Ten days later I received a letter from Dr. G. thanking me for giving up my housing allowance. I asked him where our church was on the priority list and he gave me no answer.

I immediately did a financial study to see what had happened during an approximate 7 years period. I discovered we had contributed $15,379 in cash. Utilities and other costs came to $23,779 for a total of $39,158. During the same period of time the district had paid $14,110 in housing allowance. During this period we were paying off a $100,000 bond program which hung around the church's neck, and the district's! Of course, we paid our own health insurance, life insurance, social security and other benefits that normal churches were expected to pay for the pastor. We were to end up providing a parsonage for the Church for over thirteen years.

Other events took place on the district while the latter events were going on. Pine-Grove Community had a ground-breaking on property which the district did not want. The district immediately sent out an appeal to raise money and buy yet a different property. Southwest had been funded and was having a ground-breaking. Lake Orion was having a ground-breaking.

Looking back over all these events it looked like Topsy-Turvy was well underway. It looked as if instead of the Rev. H.K. being the enemy, we were becoming the enemy!

Eastern Michigan District Minutes

(WG) Pastor's Cash Salary

Year	Cash Salary	Church	Housing Allowance
1972	$340	Clintonville	$2569
1973	0	Clintonville	2697
1974	0	Clintonville	90
1975	0	Clintonville	860
1976	0	Clintonville	1060
1977	0	Clintonville	3007
1978	0	Clintonville	3827
1979	0	Clintonville	0
1980	0	Clintonville	94
1981	0	Christ Community	94
1982	0	Christ Community	94
1983	0	Christ Community	94
1984	0	Christ Community	195
1985	0	Christ Community	0
Totals	**$340**		For 1st 7 years $14,110

1978 District Minutes Recommendations for Ministerial Support and Benevolence:
    Each church pay pastor minimum $225 per week
    Salary tied to cost of living
    All utilities paid
Social Security paid
Disability Insurance
Health Insurance
Life Insurance Minimum $10,000
Paid Vacation

We Got None of These

In the first 7 years we gave the Church $39,158 cash, utilities and other.

We provided a parsonage and house church at times for 13.5 years. This is our story. It was like climbing up a ladder. We would now move into the next phase as each year slipped by.

"Sail on! Sail on!" J. Miller

Chapter Four

802 Days

The day we gave possession of Clintonville to Mt. Zion we rejoiced. Little did we know what the next 802 days would bring to our doorstep! I went on with my school work and my wife, Marilyn went on with her art gallery.

We started out worshipping in the Wint Funeral Home. It didn't bother me, but it did bother a lot of other people. They were leaving. We were hoping that another area Nazarene church would rent or loan us space to worship in while we were building our new facility. It never happened! Following the District Superintendent's advice, we moved out of the funeral home and into our own homes.

We went through Zoning Commission battles, land options, land contracts, loans, architects, blue prints and building, with virtually no help from our Nazarene Counterparts.

The congregation had shrunk to about the size it was when we began to pastor Clintonville. We continued working, fellowshipping, and worshipping together in each others homes.

As time went on we became more and more isolated from our peers. It seemed like every possible obstacle that could be put in our way was put there. The district had taken away our housing allowance and seemingly had become obstructionist. Our major objective was our mission and the love of King Jesus. As we would invest another year of our lives we would say, "We can't give up now. We have invested too many years to fail now!" And so we kept going, going, going!

I remember at one point in our lonely journey we took our little congregation to see the play "Annie." In the days after viewing the play we would sing about the tomorrows that are only a day away. This was a source of inspiration to our little congregation. We kept working towards the goal.

We started construction of our new building in the fall of 1979. I will never forget it! First, to make the whole project "legal" we needed the blessing of the district Advisory Board. We kept moving ahead with the contractor on final arrangements to begin construction.

Day after day slipped by and I would call the District Superintendent. "Do we have the official approval yet?' "No, not yet" he would say. Finally, we were down to the wire! The earthmovers were coming the next day. I called the District Superintendent - by now I was desperate. I said, "The earthmovers are coming tomorrow. If we don't have approval from the District Advisory Board, we are going ahead anyway!" The D.S. replied, "You don't want to do that!" I said, "We don't have a choice!" Late that night, I received a phone call from the D. S. telling me that the District Advisory Board had met and granted approval for us to start the next day.

I will never forget the next day. I stood at the top of the hill where the first stage chapel would stand. As the earthmover and bulldozer moved up the new driveway, I sang "To God be the Glory, great things He has done!"

Ben Shultz, Pastor Wayne G. Greve, Rodney W. Greve, 1979

I was standing on the property as footings were being poured when a lady drove out in the field and jumped out of her car. She yelled at me, "Are you the Reverend?" I said, "I am." She said "I own this five acres next to the ten you are starting to build on and I don't want my new home next to a church!" I said, "Are you interested in selling it?" She said that she would sell it. She named a price which seemed reasonable. I didn't know where we could ever get the money. However, the next Sunday I told my little congregation about it. I said, "I don't know where we can get the money because it will take every dime we have on the new church. Someone said, "Have faith, pastor!" I said "We need five thousand dollars." In just a few minutes a handful of people raised $5,000.00. "To God be the Glory!"

Construction on the new building progressed into winter. It was a severe winter. I remember they had to put up canvas walls while they were laying bricks. We found that planning small was more difficult than planning on a larger scale. We knew the district would not help us with dollars and so we had to work within our budget.

We came up with a beautiful colonial brick chapel which would seat about 75 people. It had an office and two restrooms. The pews would be Colonial white padded with gray pearl.

Right in the middle of the interior design the district came along and wanted us to take a bunch of old used furniture from a church they were shutting down.

My church board refused the offer of used furniture. The struggle had been so long and they wanted to offer God the best. We put in the beautiful new pews. We had a white Communion Table trimmed in a natural finish on the top. The end of each pew had a cross on it. A beautiful cross graced the front wall of the sanctuary behind the white pulpit. From my own home I collected limbs from a thorn apple tree and I wove a crown of thorns to grace the top of the cross. It was a beautiful sight indeed! My wife was an interior designer and she basically planned the inside of the building. We were so happy that the years of struggle were finally coming to fruition!

So 802 days of wandering was coming to a close. A faithful handful had stayed with us as we worshipped in our homes and wandered like the Children of Israel in the wilderness. One couple even sold their home near the old church and built a new one in Goodrich, Michigan not far from the new church.

The 802 days was a real time of testing, but our God did not fail us. We would soon have a new home to worship in fit for the God we served!

"O victory in Jesus, my Saviour Forever!"
Eugene M. Bartlett, 1939

Chapter Five

Development of Christ Community

In the spring of 1980 construction was well along. At Clintonville, I had found a foundation in Texas which was designed to help home mission churches. I had written a grant to get the Clintonville parking lot blacktopped. My proposal was accepted and so we were able to blacktop the entire parking lot of Clintonville.

I knew that money was going to be tight in the construction of Christ Community, so I wrote another grant for a parking lot. This proposal was accepted like my first one was, and so we were able to pave the drive from State Highway 15 all the way up to the church, including the parking lot.

The entrance was a split entrance with two flag poles and a lovely brick sign in the middle. The sign was lighted and had a fiberglass face which could be changed should necessity dictate.

In Ortonville, where we lived, we were able to locate some large timbers. These were donated to the church. We took three timbers and built three crosses in front of the church. I designed the church's logo which consisted of three crosses with the face of Christ superimposed on them with the slogan "Per Aspera Ad Astra" underneath. This meant "Through difficulties to the stars."

Because the property had been vacant for sometime it had been used by hunters. We had to show that the property was now in use, so we built a split rail cedar fence across the front of the property. This worked and added a real touch of beauty to the property.

I lived on 5 acres of land in Ortonville, Michigan. On my land were many white pine seedlings. I transplanted these to the south line of Christ Community. Many of these are now 15 to 20 feet tall.

One day Wayne Foore, one of my members, called me and said, "Pastor, the horse farm south of the church just tore out a bunch of Lombardy poplars by the roots. Let's see if they will give them to us!" They did, and so we got a trailer and loaded them on. We brought them to Christ Community and planted them on both the north and the south lines. Later on we found some Russian Olives and planted them also.

In the development process, I discovered that one family had owned the property from 1836 - 1979. This involved four generations of the Cummings family. I thought that this was history worth noting. As far as we could determine, there had never been another building on that spot on the earth unless it was a wigwam. We felt God had reserved just that spot for His church, Christ Community! I had approached the farmer to see if he could fund a memorial in honor of his family. He agreed and did. We had a little ceremony and reporters came, took pictures and wrote it up.

My father was growing old about this time. He had been bi-vocational for 40 years as a Free Methodist minister. One of his vocations had been selling monuments and markers. He had given all his hand tools to the mission fields, but he gave some leftover granite slabs to me.

As I thought about the sacrifices that a handful of Nazarenes had made over 802 days, it seemed worthy of noting. It would be their Ebenezer. They were the Nazarene bridge builders between Clintonville and Christ Community.

To find out what an Ebenezer is, we have to go back to the book of First Samuel. The Israelites are fighting the Philistines. Previously, the Philistines had beaten them badly. Israel had asked Samuel to intercede to the Lord on their behalf. Samuel did. The scripture says in I Sam. 7:10, "The Lord thundered with a great noise that day against the Philistines, and troubled them, and they were beaten before Israel." I Sam. 7:12 says "And Samuel took a stone and set it between Mizpah and Shem, and called the name of it Ebenezer, saying, "The Lord has helped us until now[7]."

Robert Robinson wrote a hymn based on this biblical incident. The title of his hymn was, "Come, Thou Fount of Every Blessing." The second stanza reads,

> "Here I raise my Ebenezer,
> Hither by Thy help I come.
> And I hope, by Thy good pleasure,
> Safely to arrive at home.
> Jesus sought me when a stranger
> Wandering from the fold of God;
> He, to rescue me from danger,
> Interposed His precious blood."[8]

I decided to raise an Ebenezer – a holy stone of remembrance for the way the Lord had helped a small band of Nazarenes succeed for His kingdom. Across the top of the monument I had engraved a sketch of the Mackinac Bridge. The title of the monument was, "The Bridge Builders Memorial." On the monument were the names of those who participated in the 802 days.

The cornerstones were also memorial or Ebenezer stones. One read, "To God Be the Glory."

The second Ebenezer stone was for the edition the Reverend James Franklin put on the front of the chapel. I put all of Dad's granite to sacred use. These were all sacred and holy remembrances of God's goodness and the faithfulness of a small band of loyal Nazarenes.

In the spring of 1982 we started building a Commons edition on to the chapel. The congregation was growing and we needed more room. The second stage was completed August 14, 1982. The Commons had a beautiful fireplace dedicated to the Shultzs. They were the only members left who belonged to the Clintonville Church of the Nazarene. We were able to complete the second stage without borrowing any money from the banks or the district. Praise our wonderful God!

The Dedication

Left to Right: Wayne Foore, Pastor Wayne Greve, Rev. William Greve, Rodney W Greve, Rev. William Wilhoyte, Rev. Joyce Hughes, and Dr. Donald Gibson. All of the above are deceased except for the author and his son.

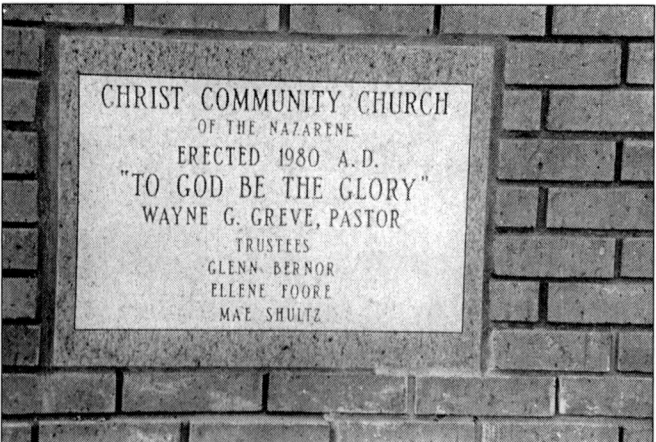

John Campbell leading the singing &
The Cornerstone

Pastor and parents William and Leeta Greve at the dedication & Christ Community

Front Entrance off Hwy. M-15

Pastor Wayne G. Greve &
Our son Rodney W Greve

Topsy Turvy in The Church of the Nazarene

Newspaper article on Ground Breaking

Newspaper article on monument dedication

Eastern Michigan District Tidings on Mortgage Burning

Christ Community Church Dedicated

On September 19 Christ Community dedicated its new commons wing with Dr. Don Gibson officiating. The same day they started a new Sunday School. Included in the ceremony were three generations of the Greve family.

Shown in the photo (left to right) Wayne Foore, Wayne G. Greve, pastor, Rev. William Greve, Rodney Greve, Rev. William Wilhoyte, Evangelist Joyce Hughes, and Dr. Don Gibson.

Christ Community just experienced a gracious revival and moving of the Holy Spirit under the ministry of the Rev. Joyce Hughes from Dover, TN. Mrs. Hughes is the daughter of the Rev. Archie Woodward. She came prayed up and preached each night under the annointing of the Holy Spirit.

EASTERN MICHIGAN DISTRICT TIDINGS

The offical news medium of the Eastern Michigan District Church of the Nazarene.

DR. DONALD GIBSON
District Superintendent
6477 Burkhart Road
Howell, MI 48843
REVEREND F. GRANT CROSS
Editor
22007 Edgewood
St. Clair Shores, MI 48080

NOTICE TO POSTMASTER: The *Tidings* is published monthly except July and August in St. Clair Shores, Michigan. All form notices for change of address or discontinuance should be returned to the editor at the above address SECOND CLASS MAIL, postage paid at St. Clair Shores, Michigan 48080.

Eastern Michigan District Tidings on Dedication

The dedication program tells the story of Christ Community Church of the Nazarene in a nutshell.

Dedication Program Front

CHRIST COMMUNITY CHURCH OF THE NAZARENE

Building Chairman:
Wayne G. Greve

Pastor:
Wayne G. Greve

Church Boards during the construction period:

1981-82

Glenn Bernor
Mary Bennett
Ellene Foore
Mae Shultz

1982-83

Mary Bennett
Judy Clark
Cliff Edgins
Ellene Foore

Building Fund Treasurer:
Mary Bennett

Church Organist:
Marilyn Greve

Minister of Music
John Campbell

Church Pianist:
Phil Criss

Associate Pastor:
William P. Wilhoyte

Schedule of Services

Sunday School .... 9:30 a.m.
Morning Worship .... 10:30 a.m.
Evening Service .... 6:00 p.m.
Family Bible Study .... Wednesday, 7:30 p.m.

Dedication Program 2

CHRIST COMMUNITY
A
BRIEF HISTORICAL SKETCH

Christ Community Church of the Nazarene has been an Ecclesiastical Corporation for one year under its present name. However, its history goes back prior to 1944 when it was the Newberry Community Church located in the northeast corner of Waterford Township in Oakland County. In 1944 it united with the Church of the Nazarene and became the Clintonville Church of the Nazarene.

In 1972, the church went through turbulent times and lost most of its congregation. Wayne G. Greve, an educator-pastor was called to be the minister of the church.

Although the church grew in the intervening years, it never really recovered from the blow suffered in 1972. In 1976, the congregation began to explore the possibility of moving to a new location.

In 1978, the property in Waterford was sold to Mt. Zion Temple, Inc. The church now entered a period of firery trial. It was unable to buy property or find a place to worship. For several months the congregation worshipped in the Lewis Wint Funeral Home in Clarkston, Michigan. Finally, they moved to the home of Glenn and Rena Bernor of Clarkston. Occasionally they were to worship in the Wayne & Ellene Foore home in Waterford. The corporate headquarters became the pastor's home.

The quest for a new location led the congregation to select a site in Genesee County along the M-15 corridor. The property was purchased from the Horace Cummings family. The Cummings family had owned the property for four generations. This site is a fifteen acre parcel located in the geographic center of five communities where there are no Nazarene Churches.

Eight-hundred and two days after leaving the old property, the congregation set their feet on the new land and in the new first stage building. It was now February 8, 1981. The construction had gone on in some of the bitterest winter weather Michigan had ever experienced. There were many casualties in the membership through this long ordeal. However, a handful of people stayed to see the project through and remain faithful to the vision God had given. Among them were Ben & Mae Shultz, the only members surviving the turbulence of 1972. The Shultzs became key people through the church's ordeal. Ben passed away before he could see the dream of the new church fulfilled. Beatrice, his daughter came to live with her mother and joined the church to help fill her father's shoes. Is it any wonder on that first morning in the new church they sang, "THE LONG, LONG NIGHT HAS PASSED: THE MORNING BREAKS AT LAST."

The congregation now looks to a bright future with Christ at her helm. To God be the glory, Great things he has done!

The second stage fellowship hall was completed Aug. 14, 1982.

Dedication Program Brief History

DEDICATION CEREMONY

Sunday, Sept. 19, 1982, 3:00 p.m.

PRELUDE..Marilyn Greve
                                                                                             Phil Criss
PROCESSIONAL...Hymn No. 40

To every man there openeth
A Way, and Ways, and a Way.
And the High Soul climbs the High Way,
And the Low Soul gropes the Low,
And between, on the misty flats,
The rest drift to and fro.
But to every man there openeth
A High Way, and a Low.
And every man decideth
The Way his Soul shall go.   Oxenham

INVOCATION.................................Rev. William P. Wilhoyte
SOLO...John Campbell
    The 23rd Psalm
PRESENTATION OF THE BUILDING TO GOD.............Wayne Foore
ACCEPTANCE OF THE BUILDING FOR GOD................Dr. Gibson
ACCOLADES..................................Wayne G. Greve, Pastor

Let us, then, be up and doing,
With a heart for any fate;
Still achieving, still pursuing,
Learn to labor and to wait.
Longfellow

Workers: *Duaine Clark, David Clark, Wayne Foore, Ray Welch, James Welch, Rodney Greve, Mike Tucker, Robbie Tucker, and Ellene Foore*

Dedication Ceremony

Wayne Foore made the presentation of the building to God. He was to say, "Dr Gibson, friends, members and pastor of Christ Community Church of the Nazarene. Every successful institution and no less church, has at its helm a very dedicated leader! We deeply appreciate that we have such a leader here. Not only does he preach about love, faith, trust, hope, and the life of holiness, but with God's anointing touch on his life our pastor is enabled to live these virtues before his flock!"

"We are all encompassed and surrounded by miracles here this afternoon! I can assure you that without divine intervention, the Commons we dedicate this day would still be part of a cornfield. We serve a God that deals in things thought impossible and we're just old-fashioned enough to believe it! Along with Nehemiah, the pastor and people of the Congregation had not only a mind to work, but a will to give."

"God was determined that we were going to be successful in our venture because, not only did those that were personally acquainted with Him put in long hours, but those of our families and friends that haven't yet had the blood applied to their hearts, also worked doggedly toward the successful completion of this unit."

"It is our utmost desire that the Commons will serve as a place of fellowship, a place for the implementing of Christian education to augment our knowledge of His word, a place where the youth of our church may have wholesome activities. However, the Commons is just a stepping stone in the dream of this Church! We trust that on our journey it will be used for God's glory."

"Today we place our confidence in God to help us carry out the great commission! To paraphrase the statement so aptly made by our founder, P. F. Bresee, we here at Christ Community, owe the gospel to the five communities that surround our area in the same measure that we have received it."

"During World War II, a reporter asked Winston Churchill what his job was and he replied 'To wage war!' 'What is your goal?' The reporter asked. Churchill said, 'Complete victory.' You ask today what our job is here and we'll reply, 'To wage war against sin.' Ask us what our goal is and we'll say, 'For everyone that enters this house of worship to find Jesus Christ as his or her personal saviour."

"Dr. Gibson, with this consecrated commitment we present this new unit to God for His Kingdom service."

Then followed the dedicatory service.

Organ- *Marilyn Greve*
Piano- *Phil Criss*

DEDICATORY MESSAGE..................................Dr. Donald Gibson

Dr. Donald Gibson is the superintendent of the Eastern Michigan District for the Church of the Nazarene College which later bestowed the honorary Doctor of Divinity degree upon him.

Dr. Gibson has a rich and varied background of leadership and service in the Church of the Nazarene. He has pastored churches in Illinois and Wisconsin and served as district superintendent of the Wisconsin, Missouri, and Central Ohio Districts. For a period of time he served as vice-president of Olivet Nazarene College where he was in charge of field service and financial development. In Department of Evangelism where he served until he became district superintendent of the Eastern Michigan District in 1979.

ACT OF DEDICATION...Wayne G. Greve, Pastor

RODNEY W. GREVE: "Blessed be the Lord God
    of Christ Community, who hath with his hands fulfilled that which he spoke with his mouth to my father Wayne G. Greve, saying"

    "Since the day that I brought forth my people from affliction, and out of the 802 days wandering, I have not chosen a house among the people, that my name might be there."

    "But today, I have chosen Christ Community, that my name might be there; and have chosen Wayne G. Greve, to be pastor of my people at Christ Community."

PASTOR: "O Lord God of Christ Community,
there is no God like thee in the heaven, nor in the earth; which keepest convenant, and shewest mercy unto thy servants, that walk before thee with all their hearts:"

CONGREGATION: Amen!

Dedication Ceremony Continued 2

PASTOR: Have respect therefore to prayer of thy servant, and to his supplication.
O Lord my God, to hearken unto the cry and the prayer which thy servant prayeth before thee:

CONGREGATION: *Amen!*

PASTOR: "That thine eyes may be open upon this house day and night, upon the place whereof thou hast said that thou wouldest put thy name there: to hearken unto the prayer which thy servant prayeth toward this place."

CONGREGATION: *Amen!*

PASTOR: "Hearken thereforeunto the supplications of thy servant, and of thy people at Christ Community, which they shall make toward this place: hear thou from thy dwelling place, ever from heaven; and when thou hearest, forgive."

CONGREGATION: *Amen!*

PASTOR: "If my people, which are called by my name, shall humble themselves, and pray, and seek my face, and turn from their wicked ways; then will I hear from heaven, and will forgive their sin, and will heal their land."

CONGREGATION: *Amen!*
PASTOR: "For now have I chosen and sanctified this house, that my name may be there for ever: and mine eyes and mine heart shall be there perpetually."

PASTOR: "....and all the people dedicated the house of God."
CONGREGATION: *Amen!*

In unison: We, the members and friends of this Church, join in the dedication of these grounds, the new commons wing, the chapel, and the furnishings for the worship of Almighty God.

II Chron. 6: 4, 6, 7, 19, 20, 21.
7: 5, 14, 16. King James Version
Paraphrased by Pastor

HYMN OF DEDICATION..Hymn No. 440
BENEDICTION..Mr. Randall Robbins
POSTLUDE..Marilyn Greve
                                                         Phil Criss

Some hope, Some dream to cling to,
Some rainbow in the sky,
Some melody to sing to,
Some service that is high.   Autermont

Dedication Ceremony continued 3

Dedication Ceremony continued 3

THE PASTORAL FAMILY

Pastor Greve has a wide range of educational background. He holds the B.A. from Adrian College and the M.A. from Eastern Michigan University. He has done post-graduate work at Siena Heights College, Wayne State University, Michigan State University and Eastern Michigan University. He was listed in Who's Who in American Education.

He has been an elementary teacher and principal in the state of Michigan, professor of education on the faculty of Northwest Nazarene College in Nampa, Idaho, a junior high teacher in special education, director of special education, and is currently a middle school resource room teacher at West Bloomfield, Michigan.

Pastor Greve is an ordained elder in the Church of the Nazarene. The Greve family has provided a unique ministry to the church for the past ten years of their lives. Both Wayne and Marilyn lead dual roles in their busy lives. Marilyn has given unstintingly of her time to be the church organist for the last nine years and runs her own business in the village of Ortonville. She is a housewife, mother, and dedicated pastor's wife.

Rodney, the Greves' fourteen year old son, loves skiing and bicycle racing. He plays the trombone and the tuba in middle school symphonic band. In the summers, he works in his grandfather Dickerson's business in Wichita, Kansas.

The Greves bring christian dedication, integrity, industry, prayer, faith, giving, and loving care for people to their ministry.

The Pastoral Family

KEY LADY

Sarah Mae Shultz (Harden) was born in Murray City, Ohio, on July 19, 1900. She was an "A" student but never graduated from high school because of health problems. She worked as chocolate dipper at Sanders Candy Co. for some time. Her favorite color is pink.

On June 24, 1920 she married Ben Shultz. Their marriage lasted 59 years. From this union 4 daughters were born. She has 15 grandchildren and 13 great-grandchildren.

Mae became a christian at age 15 and taught Sunday School classes for 25 years. She was a member of the Hillcrest United Brethern Church in Detroit. In 1961 she joined the Clintonville Church of the Nazarene.

When Christ Community Church of the Nazarene was started in 1981, she became a charter member.

Mae has been a key person through two building programs in this church. Both times she stepped forward and provided financial assistance when it seemed that the church would be blocked from moving ahead.

Her dedication to God and to this church might be characterized by these words:

> *No vision and you perish;*
> *No ideal, and you're lost;*
> *your heart must ever cherish*
> *Some faith at any cost.*   Autermont

Key Lady Sarah Mae Shultz (Harden)

From 1982 until we resigned I brought William Wilhoyte on board as associate pastor. I was doing graduate work in St. Louis, Missouri and we were continuing to grow. Sometimes the chapel was full. Rev. Wilhoyte was an able assistant and ended up marrying the church treasurer, Mary Bennett.

In the fall of 1985 it seemed like it was time to go. We had weathered many storms and now it was "goodbye time!" The little chapel was filled almost every Sunday morning.

The Communicator, the church's newsletter, expressed our sentiments as we departed!

Christ Community Church *of the* Nazarene

Phone: (313) 636-7366
5366 S. State Road
(M-15 between Goodrich and Davison)
Goodrich, Michigan 48438

Dr. Wayne G. Greve, Pastor
Home Ph: (313) 627-2930

William P. Wilhoyte, Associate Pastor
Ph: (313) 673-6384

Church Services
Church School 9:30 A.M.
Morning Worship 10:30 A.M.
Evening Service 6:00 P.M.
Wednesday 7:30 P.M.

Christ Community Church of the Nazarene Logo

Topsy Turvy in The Church of the Nazarene

The Communicator

Vol. 13
Oct. 23, 1985

LABORS OF LOVE

For thirteen-and-a-half long years, Dr. and Mrs. Wayne G. Greve have labored faithfully as Pastor and wife of Christ Community Church. This has included the paying off of a $100,000 bond indebtedness which had accrued to the church's corporate name before Dr. Greve's arrival, purchasing a new site of fifteen acres which included two building programs, and leaving the present facility and ten acres debt-free with a value of $225,000. In addition, preaching, teaching and counseling with all the many labors that are contained in a busy ministry. SUNDAY, Oct. 6th, Dr. Greve submitted his resignation as Pastor of the church. We rejoice that their faithful labors of love will live on. They will be missed for they are greatly loved. The truth Wayne has preached and lived and the beautiful music Marilyn has rendered as church organist will continue to bless our hearts. And of course, we all love Rodney, their son, now a student at Olivet Nazarene College. Your prayers for the Greves will be greatly appreciated.

Salute Jean -- a faithful Christian

Mrs. Jean Newbern has recently experienced very serious surgery. Her beautiful Christian faith and the prayers of many have brought her safely through. She, with her husband Charles, lives at Charter Oaks in Davison. It is a pleasure and an encouragement to have them in our church fellowship - Social Worker

TITHES

You may be sure that your faithfulness in bringing in the tithes and offerings is always appreciated. After the long summer, October is filled with many needs. Let us continue to give faithfully and cheerfully - for the Lord loves a cheerful giver.

SHOWERS OF BLESSINGS

All who attended our Special Revival Services with Dr. L.S. Oliver and the Robbins were certainly recipients of many rich blessings. The wonderful preaching of Dr. Oliver and his delightful humor, plus the music of the Robbins and the music of Marilyn and Phil at the organ and piano, made every service special. Above all, the presence of the Lord was manifested in a wonderful way. To God be the glory and the honor!

WE'RE RIGHT IN THE MIDDLE
of our

Denominational wide Sunday School Drive. Only a little time left to go. Vacations are over, students are back in school, the weather is not too hot or too cold--what a perfect time for growth in our outreach. Let them know-is the emphasis! Pray, work, call and make the last Sundays count!

BEST ASSOCIATE

A salute to Pastor Bill, the best associate pastor and yoke-fellow that a man could ever have! God bless you!

CHURCH BOARD

A salute to the best church board that a pastor could ever have. Faithful, supportive, harmony & unity of purpose, visionary and real Christians!

THANKS

To Wayne Foore for painting the front doors of the church. To Richard Pifer for working long and hard to solve the parking lot light problem.

LAST POTLUCK

Nov. 3rd, following the morning worship service. Hostess, Mrs. Hecht.

THE FUTURE

AS BRIGHT AS THE PROMISES OF GOD!

The Communicator

The Pastor's Thoughts

RELIEVING GUARD

Came the Relief. "What, Sentry, ho!
  How passed the night through the long waking?"
"Cold, cheerless, dark--as may befit
  The hour before the dawn is breaking."

"No sight? no sound?" "No;nothing save
  The plover from the marshes calling,
And in yon western sky, about
  An hour ago, a star was falling."

"A star? There's nothing strange in that."
  "No, nothing; but, above the thicket,
Somehow it seemed to me that GOD
  Somewhere had just relieved a picket."

—Francis Bret Harte.

Dr. Wayne G. Greve

In our fourteenth year, the above says it all for Wayne, Marilyn & Rodney Greve! Good bye! Fond farewell to all our friends and members at Christ Community Nazarene. May God be with you as you carry on "HIS DREAM!"

The Pastor's Thoughts and Ben and Mae Shultz Memorial Fireplace

"And my people shall dwell in a peaceable home, and in secure dwellings and quiet resting places." Isa. 32:18

Chapter Six

Years Following Christ Community
1985-1989

We were never offered another church. At the time we thought it was strange, but looking back we were to see divine providence involved and at work! I plunged into educational work with all my heart and Marilyn continued with her art gallery. Since we lived in Ortonville, Michigan we ended up attending the Lake Louise Church of the Nazarene. I would preach occasionally and Marilyn would play.

In 1988 we decided we needed better routes to work and so we built a home in Clarkston, Michigan closer to my work and giving Marilyn freeway access to her work. We continued going to Lake Louise for awhile. However, we needed shorter commuting distance to church so we chose to go to Hillcrest Church of the Nazarene. Later, it would be called Silver Lake. I was asked to teach a Sunday School Class and Marilyn was asked to play the organ.

Things were going well. One day as I was teaching a young married person began to deride what I was saying. I talked the situation over with my wife and we concluded that we had had enough with attitudes in our church. Meeting with the pastor we told him we did not want to be the cause of trouble. We quoted Matt. 10:14, 15 which says, "And whosoever shall not receive you, nor hear your words, when you leave that house or that city, shake off the dust from your feet." [9]

Today, the March, 2009 statistics indicate that Hillcrest (Silver Lake) which was a strong church when we were there, is now running 11 in Sunday School and 48 in morning worship. We left because we did not want to be the cause of trouble and we followed Matthew's admonition.

I grew up a Free Methodist. Dad was a Free Methodist minister for 40 years. We were close to a strong Free Methodist Church so we started going there. We left our membership in the Church of the Nazarene. One of my friends in CFM was a Free Methodist music director. He had spent several years directing music at Williams Lake Church of the Nazarene. He had finally left and came back to the Free Methodist Church. S.A. from that church later became D. S. of Eastern Michigan Nazarene District.

While there I was asked to teach a Sunday School Class and occasionally asked to fill the pulpit. As my teaching progressed, I became suspicious about various concepts the publishers were promoting. I called them and asked a few questions. Then I asked the main question I called them about, "Are you Calvinists?" The reply was, "Yes, we are but don't we hide it well?" Free Methodists are not supposed to be Calvinists! I never said a word to the local church. I just modified the lessons when I needed to.

My wife and I started a small care group at this church while we were there. This group is still functioning today. We found the Free Methodists were not nearly as friendly as Nazarenes. We also found that the power structure was still largely dominated by one family. Two generations of one family had been the District Superintendents of the Eastern Michigan District of the Free Methodist Church. The third generation ended up with a position in general headquarters of the Free Methodist Church. We were there five or six years and did make some lasting friends.

On June 14, 1994 I retired from teaching. That day they wheeled into the gymnasium a blue spruce to be planted in my honor. Eight hundred people gave me a standing ovation. I had taught for over thirty-six years in public education. In the fall of that year I suffered a massive heart attack, but God spared me. I went on as a substitute teacher in the public schools of two states through 2009.

My retirement from public education brought a great healing time in my life. I first purchased 20 acres in Arenac County. This was not far from where my grandparents had lived and died. We built a small rustic cabin there. We had to carry in water and we had an old fashioned outhouse. My boy collected several deer there with his bow and he loved it!

We named this property Chippewa Place after an Indian Tribe. We planted trees and had a great time until we discovered that we were in a high crime area. Vandals set fires, one of which burned right to the door of our cabin. It was only the DNR that saved it! Then we were stolen blind. Our friends' relatives had their parents murdered!

We decided to sell the property. First, we sold it on a land contract, and then we sold the land contract. I spent days searching for property on the west side of Michigan. Eventually, I found a piece. It was 70 acres on the south edge of Kalkaska County and not far from Traverse City. It was on a blacktop road but had no buildings.

This was where I had my first heart attack. As soon as I recovered, I completed the purchase of the property. Next, I started building. I first had erected a Morton pole barn. I put in electricity and a phone. This was completed in the fall. The next year I bought a house trailer and lived in it for 100 days with my yellow Lab, Thunder. We lived there while I supervised the construction of a two story home. I would go home on week-ends.

We owned this place for ten years and named it Whispering Timber based on local Indian legends about the Manistee River. Also, because I had nearly died here with a heart attack, the name involved a great hymn <u>Whispering Hope.</u>

The land had deer, bear, coyotes, raccoons, grouse, ducks, geese, beavers, wildcats and other animals. In short we had almost every animal that lives in Michigan on our property.

I bought a little 4 cylinder diesel tractor. This proved to be an invaluable tool around the property. I brought in a bulldozer and bulldozed out timber to create fields and trails. I planted deer food in the fields. The deer came and lots of other game. This proved to be very therapeutic. I loved the smell of new turned soil and new mown hay. Over the ten years we owned the property we brought many friends to share the joys of Whispering Timber. Later I bought a heavy duty golf cart which would carry four passengers up some of the steep hills on the property. We were enjoying life immensely.

A lot of healing was taking place from our thirteen and a half years at Clintonville and Christ Community. In the meantime we sold our home in Clarkston, Michigan and moved to Indiana where my wife was born.

Whispering Timber
Top: Starting the Pole Barn
Bottom: Home Under Construction

Whispering Timber
Top: Inside
Bottom: Friends for the fourth of July

Whispering Timber
Top: On Our Boat at Fife Lake
Bottom: Wayne, Dave, Thunder: with our bucks

Whispering Timber
Wayne and Thunder: Pals Forever
Wayne and Thunder: Chapel at the Pine

Whispering Timber
Top: Thunder in his favorite habitat
Bottom: Thunder retrieving a duck

Top: Field of Dreams Whispering Timber
Bottom: Building our bridge. David Jewel, Roger Pratt, myself and Thunder

Top: My Son Rodney and myself with a trophy steelhead from the mighty Manistee River
Bottom: Guide Chuck Scribner and myself with my trophy steelhead trout on the Manistee River

Whispering Timber
Top: Rodney Greve with button horn buck taken
with a bow. Thunder examining
Bottom: Last major project: The pond at Whispering Timber
Now we would be seven and a half hours from Whispering Timber.
Still a lot of healing was going on. I loved being a "pioneer" and
developing the place from the ground up.

"Topsy Turvy is a reality – not a state of mind.". WG

Chapter Seven

Early years at First Church
1999-2002

In 1999, my wife retired and sold her art gallery in Flint, Michigan. "I want to move to Indiana where I was born. I want to attend First Church in Indianapolis. My grandparents and parents all attended there. If we go there we will be the third generation to attend!"

So, we sold our home in Clarkston, Michigan and moved to Indiana. We moved about nine miles east of First Church. The drive to the cabin would now be 7 to 7 ½ hours long. We were able to live there summers and through November. Then we would come home and I would substitute teach for the rest of the year.

I shortly requested that my ministerial credentials be transferred from Eastern Michigan to the Indianapolis District. This is a letter I received from the D.S. The e-mail list mentioned in the letter never happened or if it did it was short-lived. (enclosure, letter May 26, 1999.)

STEPHEN T. ANTHONY
District Superintendent

JAMES L. EWERS
Administrative Assistant

May 26, 1999

Rev. Wayne & Marilyn Greve
671 S. Brune Ct.
New Palestine, IN 46163

Dear Wayne & Marilyn:

A couple of weeks ago I received a note from you that you had requested your credentials to be transferred to the Indianapolis District. I have been meaning to write you and have just received your change of address card. We have taken action to make the necessary change regarding your credentials; however, I want you to know how much we're going to miss you on the Eastern Michigan District.

Over the last several years, we haven't had a lot of contact; however, when we have it has been good. I trust that God will give you good days. Drop me a note sometime and let me know what's happening in your lives. Once again, thanks for sending along the information. I'll continue to keep you on our E-mail newsletter list, Wayne. May God's richest blessing be yours.

In His Service,

Stephen Anthony/mld

Stephen T. Anthony
District Superintendent

STA:mld

The people at First Church were very warm and friendly. My wife had family there and in the city. We felt like we were in heaven on earth. The Church was thriving. We heard great music every Sunday and good sermons.

Hoosiers love to eat out. We went out a lot with different friends on a regular basis. We enjoyed the cuisine of Indiana. We met in each others homes to play cards and fellowship. Together, we went to gospel concerts, fairs, museums and theaters. We were fully enjoying life in a large church and a large city.

I was asked often to teach Sunday School. I taught children and adults. People always seemed to enjoy my lessons. I had applied for and was granted a lifetime certificate to teach in Indiana. I was substituting in three or four public school systems. Most of the kids loved me. Our lives were very busy and we felt fulfilled!

Sometime in January of 2000 I had an interchange with the Eastern Michigan District Superintendent. This was what he wrote. (letter of January 26, 2000.)

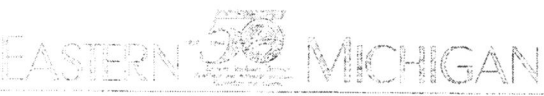

January 26, 2000

Rev. Wayne Greve
671 S. Brune Ct.
New Palestine, IN 46163

Dear Wayne:

It certainly was good to receive a letter from you. I trust that you and Marilyn are doing well and enjoying your new home in Indiana. Please know that you are missed on the Eastern Michigan District.

Thank you for sending along the information regarding Clintonville and Christ Community. I know that you poured a lot of your heart and soul into this relocation. I wasn't aware of all the disappointments you had along the way but I certainly appreciate all that you did to get the church where it is today.

Just to update you a little as to where the church is as of today. This week, the pastor has resigned and I have plans to bring a new pastor in and to restart this congregation. I don't know if there's much left or that any of those that were there will come back; however, I do believe that it's a great location and a very fine building and should be a strong church for the future. I'm asking the district to put significant money into helping us get a quality pastor and also looking toward acquiring a parsonage.

Wayne, would you and Marilyn please be so kind as to pray for us. I know that we can't go back and undo some of the things in the past; however, even in the bad things of the past, God uses them for His purpose in the future. I was reading just the other day the story of Joseph in Genesis and it reminded me that while he did not understand everything at the time, God was using him every step of the way. I believe God has used you in this way and the foundation you have laid for Christ Community will prove to be very fruitful for the coming years.

If you are ever up in this area, please feel free to contact me. I would like to sit down and have a coffee with you. May God's richest blessing be yours.

In His Service,

Stephen T. Anthony
District Superintendent

STA/mld

Things in Michigan were about to change. By this time Christ Community had had two pastors. My successor had done well and had tried to follow the vision of the people and myself. However, number two after me was a lady who made shipwreck. More about that in the next chapter. Here at First Church Indianapolis we were treated better as Nazarenes than anywhere we had ever been, except for my tenure at Northwest Nazarene College in Nampa, Idaho. There Dr. John Riley was a superb leader!

I must add that over the years we had very cordial relationships with Dr. S.A. We were also developing good relations with T.L. on the Indianapolis District.

We don't know what happened or why. We only know that our ministry is fractured like a number of other people's. Our lives are forever changed. We are now <u>exiles</u> from our own church which we served faithfully for over 50 years.

"... *Behold all things are become new.*" *II Cor. 5:17*

Chapter Eight

Christ Community Becomes Crossroads
2001-2002

My successor at Christ Community was an educator-pastor like myself, by the name of J.F. He faithfully stayed with the dream and added to the front of the church keeping the architectural style of the building. He also added a partial basement.

My second successor was a lady, P.Q. She tried to stay with the dream by getting a $100,000 loan from someone in Texas. She built a large addition on the church.

Sometime during her ministry things started to go astray. Certain members in the congregation informed the D.S. that things were slipping with their pastor. They were ignored! Then came the big blowup, a huge moral problem was discovered. The church blew apart. The D S. stepped in and shut the church down.

The church reopened after about a year under the name of Crossroads. It was still Nazarene as everyone knew in the community. Some of my former members attended the opening service. They reported to me in tears that they were dumbfounded when the new pastor took the credit for founding the church. I tried to console them at the time.

Apparently, founding was now interpreted as changing the name. Land acquisition, zoning commissions, contractors, blueprints, and everything which goes along with a real founding had been compressed into "name change!"

After hearing what was going on up in Michigan I did write a letter apparently to both D. S'. Here are excerpts from the two responses I got at that time.

I received an e-mail from S.A. in Michigan. This was on April 21, 2001.

"Wayne, wanted to let you know that Christ Community, now Crossroads, had 170 on Easter Sunday. They are doing really well and many have found Christ as Saviour. They have doubled the parking lot again and are already beginning to talk about a new sanctuary. Thought you would like to know. Thanks for your vision, sacrifice, and hard work. None of this would be possible had you not made the move you did years ago to this location . . ." S.A.

Since I knew both the District Superintendents I had written my concerns to my own D. S. Here is an excerpt from a letter I received from my D.S. in Indiana. It is dated May 2, 2001 so it came the next month after the e-mail from Michigan.

Dear Wayne & Marilyn . . .

Wayne, . . . you and Marilyn are now clipping coupons for the excellent work that you gave at Christ Community which is now called Crossroads Church of the Nazarene . . . Your thirteen years of hard labor in loving and building the Kingdom of God did not go in vain." Sincerely, T.R.L.

Having heard many things about what was going on up there, I decided to make a visit. On the morning of June 6, 2002 I paid a visit to the campus of Crossroads (Christ Community).

In the Bible, stones and trees were markers or memorials for covenants with God. In Joshua, Chapter 4 we find the record of twelve stones set up as a memorial for God's miraculous grace in parting the waters of Jordan and allowing the people to pass over.

We had placed granite markers in various locations which told the story of the church. I found every covenant stone had been hammered to pieces or carted away. Only the historical monument was in one piece and laying in a field behind the church. Even the

Cornerstone Covenants were gone. I couldn't get inside the church so I did not know what happened inside! The three crosses were torn down and gone. Only a sidewalk, footing and a tree were left where the Bridge Builders Memorial had stood. The original sign, which could have been used, was broken up and hauled out back of the church.

The historical record in stone and covenants of a small group of people, who fought desperately to save a Nazarene Church, and the records in stone, of God's Covenant grace had been annihilated!

Now we know how the Israelites felt when other nations tore down the temple and carted away the sacred elements. But worse, this was our own church family! I wondered why they didn't cut down the trees, now about 20 feet tall. They were seedlings which I had transplanted from my own place in Ortonville.

The trees were the only reminders of God's Covenants between Him and a small group of loyal Nazarenes trying to bring order out of chaos! Yes, modern Nazarene vandals had obliterated history rather completely!

It was not until Nov. 15, 2009 that I would learn what happened to the inside of the church. On the way to my boy's home, I noticed a bright red car which looked like a sports car. A man and woman were getting out of the car. I hit my brakes and turned into the parking lot. I got out of my car and started walking up to them. I introduced myself and the gentleman told me that he was the Assistant District Superintendent of the Eastern Michigan District.

I asked if I could see the inside of the church and he responded that I could. The first thing I noticed was that the chapel was completely gutted and made into a playpen for kids. The beautiful white pews, communion table, pulpit and cross were gone. Now I knew what Pastor W.W's wife meant when in casual conversation, at a social event, she mentioned "gutting that church." The beautiful fellowship kitchen was all chopped up with partitions. The addition put up by P.Q. was now a temporary worship center with portable chairs. The Covenant stone honoring Ben and Mae Shultz was still in the fireplace. It was the only thing left.

I asked the assistant about the monuments. He knew nothing. I explained to him. He said he would like to see the one on its back out in the field. I showed it to him. He told me that they planned to restart the church which was dead again!

When confronted about his actions of destruction, the Rev. W.W. was to say, "We don't pay homage to the past!" Oh! What about Pilot Point? What about Bresee? What about many other histories in our hundred years?

I had always thought our church was founded on the Rock, but I guess "sinking sand" would be a better description! Maybe this bent to destruction started when a historical untruth appeared in the District Minutes which stated that Christ Community was founded in 1945. Anyone who knows anything about the history of Christ Community knows that it was founded in 1980, 802 days after the death of Clintonville.

The D.S. and the D.A.B. were delinquent in never taking the initiative to disorganize Clintonville. They hung the name on Christ Community like an albatross around her neck. Now they proceeded to destroy her piece by piece!

"Humpty Dumpty sat on a wall,
Humpty Dumpty took a great fall,
All the king's horses and all the king's men
Couldn't put Humpty together again."
Nursery Rhyme

Chapter Nine

First Church From 2002-2008

Things were going well at First Church in 2002 and beyond. In about 2003 I was asked to write a column for the First Church Newsletter. The news letter was called "First Church News." My column was called, "A Senior Moment." What follows is an example.

May 2003 · First Church Memo

A SENIOR MOMENT . . .
Dr. Wayne Greve

Marrying a wife is quite an adventure! When I married Marilyn, she was a city girl with little knowledge of country ways. I grew up in northern Michigan on the end of a fly rod. One of my favorite pastimes was fly-fishing for trout.

Dad had a secret hideaway in Crawford County which had a stream that was not very accessible to the public. The stream was full of pink-meated brook trout.

I introduced Marilyn to a family tradition of trout for breakfast. Trout or "brookies" were easy to prepare. I simply cut off the heads, zipped out the entrails, gave them a wash, and they were then ready for the cooking process.

Cooking consisted of heating a huge cast iron frying pan, rolling each fish in flour, wrapping each fish with a strip of bacon, adding a dash of pepper, and cooking at medium heat. The fish were served with toast, honey, and sometimes fried potatoes. Of course, a fresh pot of coffee topped off the process!

I always said those meals were "fit for a king." In fact, they were occasions of deep family fellowship which I equated with the post-resurrection appearance of Jesus to the seven fishing disciples (John 21:1-24). Jesus seemed to be gone, and Peter said, "I am going fishing!" Six of the disciples said that they were going with Him. They fished all night and caught nothing.

When morning broke and they approached the shore, a stranger asked, "Have you caught anything?" The disciples answered, No!" Jesus said, "Cast your net on the right side of the ship." We all know the result! Then John said, "It is the Lord!"

What marvelous words of recognition! As they came to land, they saw a fire of glowing coals and fish laid on it with bread. Then King Jesus said, "Come and dine." Is this fellowship?

What a day that will be when Jesus says to us, "Come and dine."

One day a "Senior Moment" and the whole paper were trashed as soon as I walked off campus for the summer. I had worked hard to write in advance, columns for the whole summer. I was told that the pastor decided to go in a different direction. No different direction ever emerged. The paper my column was in came to an untimely death!

Also at this time I started participating in a prayer time with the pastor preceding morning worship. This custom was to continue for a number of years.

Although I was an ordained elder in the Church of the Nazarene, we were required to attend the membership class taught by the pastor. This was required of us before we could join the church. We never did understand this but obediently complied.

In 2004 mass departures of staff members began to occur at First Church. This was disconcerting but I believe a harbinger of what was ahead. In the fall of '04 the pastor asked me if I would become curriculum consultant for the adult Sunday School. I agreed and immediately I launched a study of the adult Sunday School Classes. It would take me about three months to complete the study. I filed my report with the church Board on January 5, 2005

I discovered that out of 12 classes only about 2½ classes were using the designated materials recommended by the Church of the Nazarene. There were a number of other concerns that needed to be addressed. Subsequently, my report was bumped around and occasionally discussed until finally it was deep-sixed and nothing ever happened!

Meanwhile, new staff members began to arrive in 2005 while others here in 2004 began to depart. It was obvious that things were going astray.

Among the departing staff was T.J. First Church gave him people and money to start a new church. I thought that this was a wonderful gesture on the part of the church.

Near the end of 2005 I was asked and agreed to take over the mid-week service which had dwindled to 12 or 15 people in attendance. I was told I would be given $25 a week in compensation. Until my departure in 2009 I never received a penny of compensation for conducting the midweek service.

In the meantime I had also been elected to the Board of Christian Life. Although my Sunday School report would surface a number of times in the coming months, it gradually died a slow and lingering death here too!

With my wife, M. J. on the organ and consistent, advanced planning the midweek service began to grow. In fact many times attendance soared to over one hundred. Then they asked us for advanced scheduling on the internet. The job began to take more time and energy. I never complained. After all, I was doing the Lord's work!

As we worked our way into '06 and '07 M.L. began to change, the church began to change. There seemed to be more conflict over many things. M.L. never supported the midweek service in any noticeable way. He came once or twice that I remember.

We had an organ at our home in northern Michigan. One day we decided that it was not used enough there, so we gave it to the church to be used in prayer meeting. It was never even acknowledged by the pastor.

We had our Senior Pastor at our home for dinner more than once. It was never acknowledged. It was like we owed these courtesies to them. When the Senior Pastor's daughter graduated from high school they held an open house. We were never invited although many of our friends were. We sent his daughter a check. It was never acknowledged. We never knew why.

It seemed now, that every improvement we tried to make in the midweek service was being met with a subtle resistance. We had lots of hard of hearing people in our services and an inadequate sound system. We asked for help but couldn't get it! Finally, we got together and raised the money among ourselves to buy something more adequate.

We had a good sound man, but frequently we came to church to discover that the pastor had appropriated him. This left us with no one to run the sound system. Yet, we were expected to record the service for shut-ins. We were never told this in advance so we could plan.

As I said, we were being recorded for a tape ministry going to shut-ins. I discovered that the tapes were also being sent to the D. S.

I assumed so we could be monitored. I don't know if this was to see if we were subversive or what.

In 2007 the church was celebrating its centennial. They published a wonderful book of pictures about people and events. You can't find a picture of the midweek service, or activities or about the people. You cannot find a single mention about our hard work. There were a lot of things about sports and other kinds of events. Lest the reader think we are being petty, I don't think we are. We never asked for special treatment, only equal treatment!

Also, in 2006 I wrote the editor of Holiness Today. I also wrote the general superintendents with concerns about our church. There were others who wrote too. I lift one paragraph from the editor's response to me. "From where I sit, there are numerous battles shaping up that have serious implications for our Zion. I trust we will never concede the authority of scripture, the omniscience of God, and the message of heart purity to the objectors of such doctrines." David J. Felter, Editor in Chief.

In 2007 the senior pastor became very sick. First Church was now in a valley. Pulpit work was passed off to associates. Some were young and inexperienced. I tried to hold steady with the work of prayer meeting and the Board of Christian Life. In spite of this staff was coming and going. People were being hurt. Things were beginning to spin out of control!

The following is an example of what happened to staffing patterns at First Church over a five year period of time. The coming of the "prince" created even more turmoil and change.

First Church Staff Arrivals and Departures

Position	**Years**
Adult and Evangelism (T.J.)	still on board 2004
Business Administrator (D.A.)	gone 2004
Community Life Pastor (Tr. J.)	gone 2004
Children's Minister (H.D.)	gone 2004
Music Pastor (Mc.T.)	still on board 2004
Senior Pastor (M.L.)	still on board 2004
Assistant Pastor (T.J.)	gone 2005

Music Pastor (Mc.T.)	gone 2005
Business Administrator (P.D.)	on board 2005
Calling Associate (H.J.)	on board 2005
Youth Pastor (P.S.)	on board 2005
Senior Pastor (M.L.)	on board 2005
Assimilation Pastor (L.D.)	on board 2006
Business Administrator (P.D.)	on board 2006
Children's Minister (B.Z.)	on board 2006
Music Minister (B.T.)	on board 2006
Next Generation Pastor (H.T.)	on board 2006
Senior Pastor (M.L).	on board 2006
Business Administrator (P.D.)	on board 2007
Music Pastor (B.T.)	on board 2007
Associate Pastor (L.D.)	on board 2007
Children's Pastor (B.Z.)	on board 2007
Senior Pastor (M.L.)	gone 2008
Youth Pastor (P.S.)	on board 2007
Associate Pastor (L.D.)	on board 2008
Children's Pastor (B.Z.)	on board 2008-09
Music Pastor (T.B.)	on board 2008
Business Administrator (P.D.)	on board 2008-09
Senior Pastor (W.W.)	on board 2008-09
Youth Pastor (P.S.)	on board 2008-09
Associate Pastor (L.D.)	gone 2009
Business Administrator (P.D.)	gone 2009
Children's Pastor (B.Z.)	gone 2009
Music Pastor (T.B.)	gone 2009
Visitation Pastor – interim (W.G.)	gone 2009
Music Pastor - interim (B.A.)	on board 2009
Youth Pastor (P.S.)	on board 2009 gone
Visitation Pastor (C.J.)	on board 2009
Children's Pastor (B.J.)	on board 2009
Middle School Pastor (Cr.J.)	on board 2009
Youth Pastor (P.S.)	gone Sept. 2009

Twenty one staff changes in a five year period including senior pastors. Others with above; Sound man (H.S). Nursery Director and staff forced out.

This is unconscionable in a First Church where one would expect to find solidarity, continuity and other features of lasting value. Associates seem to be treated as expendable resources.

Now I have this dream. I have gone to a convention in a large city. I am lost from my group. I am alone and wandering. I stagger through piles of slag, rusting down steel structures that were once buildings. I am carrying a huge pile of material. In desperation I start pitching it into the rubble of the city.

As I wander I realize that this city has been hit with a nuclear bomb! Hopelessly, I understand that I can do nothing! I awaken and realize that I have been cleaning out my closet!

In my closet are rows of satchels and zipper notebooks which are full of some minister's ideas to make First Church into a mega-church. These never happened. Piles of ideas about Sunday School discipleship, growth patterns, etc. These ideas are discarded as the leaders move from one idea to the next. Piles of Sunday School material never used. Teacher training schemes which never happened! Curriculum studies that were "deep-sixed" by the board. Everyone is on a different page! In one year our church went through Grove City, Willow Creek, and Purpose Driven programs. In the end we never did any of these programs! Is it getting Topsy Turvy? Apparently, someone didn't hear the D.S.' report of 2000 on p. 64 of the district minutes! It decried the latter.

"Renovere" came along, there was one conference. It too disappeared. Also, I am doomed to forever getting literature about it through the mail. Does anyone know where we are going?

There was the Sunday School Teacher Installation Service. I was asked to recruit substitutes. I came up with twenty-one teachers. I then asked the Board of Christian Life, "If we could have an installation service?" The powers that be agreed to it. The Nazarene Manual has a model for one. When the ceremony came the pastor skipped over most of the important vows. The Sunday School Superintendent got lost in the installation service. He mixed the substitutes with regular teachers and part of the substitutes never did get installed! Yes, everything is going Topsy Turvy!

Last spring we finished our first revival with the new "prince." He immediately called his former D.S. to be the evangelist. The "prince" then decided to mix the revival with a "Faith Promise Convention." Faith Promise is the way Nazarenes raise money for missions. When the revival was over, no one that I saw or heard about had been saved or sanctified. The "prince" got up the next Sunday and said, "We have finished a wonderful revival!" Everyone that had a brain just went away shaking their heads! Yes, we are Topsy Turvy.

In 2008, we were featured on the front page of the Indianapolis District Nazarene. We were featured along with special friends of the D.S. For the coming banquet we are not invited, (2009). Special friends for several years, retired and trashed all in one year! We can only hope that God doesn't work that way!

"It is better to trust in the Lord than to trust in princes." Psalm 118:9

Chapter Ten

The Prince Arrives

In the fall of 2008 the pastor M.L. at First Church had an extended illness. Before this things had not been going well. During his illness no one knew if the pastor would recover. After numbers of meetings with the D.S. and First Church Board, M.L. submitted his resignation. This brought many shock waves to the church. Attendance fell. There were major concerns. The church was also involved in the music wars that were sweeping the country.

The church immediately set out to search for a new pastor. Because of the uncertainties the church had endured, it seemed imperative that they needed to select a new pastor as soon as possible.

After several candidates interviewed with the Board, the D.S. skillfully maneuvered the Rev. W.W. to the forefront. He and the D.S. from Eastern Michigan worked in tandem behind the scenes. They were able to elicit a 100% vote of confidence from the Board to call the Rev. W.W. The Rev. W.W. was as smooth as a ribbon in his interviews. He gave the Board just what they wanted to hear. He was smooth as silk before the congregation too! When it came time for the congregational vote it came in at 97% for the Rev. W.W. With all the talk around First Church it appeared that these events must signify God's will.

Although I knew about events at Christ Community in Michigan, I decided to bury them. Even though the wounds were very deep, this was a nice pastor, I would forgive and forget. In 2001, I had expressed my concerns to the two district superintendents whom I knew; one was supposedly my friend; the other was involved in the situation at Christ Community. I had been a fellow traveler with him in Michigan before I came to Indiana. I shared the exchange of letters that took place in 2001 between myself and both District Superintendents in Chapter nine. I had briefed them on the price my wife and I had paid to give birth to Christ Community. They had written letters of reassurance to me.

The "prince" arrived at First Church in the fall of 2008. He started small.

1. He tore down the staff parking signs, stating that there would be no preference not even for himself. He would park out by the dumpster if he had to. (I never saw his vehicle by the dumpster, it was always parked in the senior pastor's old spot.) But, he made an impression on the congregation. They said, "This is a real regular guy."
2. He took out the big conference room table and made it his very large office. According to my minority interviews, he did the same thing at Rockfield only he added a private shower and toilet. This remodel cost approximately $90,000 at Rockfield, according to interviewees.
3. He changed the platform and the pulpit.
4. He added a permanent cross to the front wall above the choir loft.
5. He changed the bulletins to Flint Central Church style.
6. He modeled the worship services after Flint Central. (This was the largest church on the Eastern Michigan District where he came from.)

The events which I describe are outlined in "The Prince" by Machiavelli. "Hence we may learn the lesson that on seizing a state (church) the usurper (new minister) should bethink him of all the injuries he must inflict, and inflict them all at a stroke, that he may not have to renew them daily, but be enabled by their discontinuance to reassure men's minds, and win them by benefits."[10] The initial benefits would be flattery and pandering to individuals and to the congregation. After he forced a few staff members out he stopped the exit interviews with the board.

The "prince" started small to make his presence felt. However, he would rise higher. About the middle of December he announced that he was keeping all the staff. He said and did this while behind the scenes he was setting the stage to get rid of everyone that he perceived might stand in his way. The congregation was so happy because many loved their staff. However, this was just the beginning of what would happen to staff people.

1. Shortly, after this the music minister and the assimilation pastor suddenly resigned. The music minister position is a major one in Nazarene Churches. It probably runs right behind senior pastor in importance. The choir was upset and so were many in the congregation.
2. Shortly after this the sound man left.
3. The Administration Council was eliminated.
4. Next he worked on forcing out the nursery director and staff.
5. Forced out the calling pastor (me).
6. Fired the children's minister and the executive pastor. (All of the above after he said he was keeping them.)
7. He put in a local man as interim music pastor.
8. He hired a young man from Michigan and created a new position for him. To do this he took middle school ministry away from the current youth pastor. The new position was called middle school and recreation pastor. This young man seemed to be the "prince's" shirttail buddy from Michigan.
9. Since neither youth pastor had enough to do, they were assigned calling duties which overlapped into my area of responsibility.
10. After firing the current children's minister he hired his former children's minister from Rockfield Church of the Nazarene.
11. After I was forced out he hired another buddy who came from Michigan at the same time the "prince" came to First

Church. C.J. had a split occur in the church he pastored for one year. He had also pastored Rockfield and helped plant Armadillo Nazarene where the new middle school man had come from. So another buddy was now in place!
12. Finally, the original youth minister saw what was happening and decided to get another job. This put the young man from Armadillo in the saddle.
13. Lastly, after months of interim the "prince" made the local minister of music permanent.

Now the slate was completely clean. The "prince's" master plan was full-blown. How did all this happen? Machiavelli describes it well. "To rely wholly on the lion is unwise; and for this reason a prudent prince (minister) neither can nor ought to keep his word when to keep it is hurtful to him and the causes which led him to pledge it are removed . . . no prince (minister) was ever at a loss for plausible reasons to cloak a breach of faith . . ."[11]

It is necessary, indeed, to put a good colour on this nature, and to be skilful in feigning and dissembling. But men are so simple, and governed so absolutely by their present needs, that he who wishes to deceive will never fail in finding willing dupes."

In juxtaposition to this the prophet Isaiah in his 59th chapter would utter this complaint, "None calls for justice, nor does anyone plead for truth; they trust in vanity and speak lies. They conceive mischief and bring forth iniquity."[12]

". . . justice is far from us; . . . we wait for light, but behold darkness; for brightness, but we walk in deep shadows."[13]

". . . justice is driven backward, and righteousness stands afar off; for truth has fallen in the street, and uprightness cannot enter."[14]

"Up until events started to unravel with me personally I had the utmost confidence and belief in the pastor. I thought I had found a new friend who would believe in me and what I could do for God.

On January 5, I met with the Rev. W.W. for a discussion on expanding my duties. I had already managed the midweek service for four years. We met at Starbucks on 75th Street.

The topic under discussion was an expansion of my duties. I already had offered to resign my duties with the midweek. However, he stated that he wanted me to continue in the position. We discussed visitation pastor or chaplain and what it would entail. I was led to believe that it would be a full time position. I told pastor that we were going to Florida about the 17th of January. He said, "When you get back, come in and go to work."

On January 30, 2009 I had a brief meeting with the pastor. On February 2, I was presented with a contract. I was shocked, I thought it would be a year's contract. Instead, it was called interim for 90 days. I remember expressing my apprehension about interim contracts. I cited my experience in Michigan where I had gone through two interim contracts. They both ended with the D.S. placing his two sons-in-law as pastors of these churches.

I remember thinking, "I don't know the reason for this sudden switch while we were in Florida, but the Rev. W.W. is a very trustworthy gentleman." So I went ahead and signed the contract. After I signed the contract the "prince" looked at me and blurted out, "How do I get rid of P.D.?" I was dumb-founded! I thought church was a place of brotherly love. I responded with some lame duck answer to his question. I know it was inappropriate, but I was very shocked at the question. Next, he started in on N. & B.Z. "Have you heard the story about them?" By now my brain was working again. I said, "I don't want to hear the story about them." He didn't say any more. I went to work throwing my heart and soul into the job.

On April 9, we met with Dr. T.L. and his wife B. During the course of the dinner conversation, he would remark that he was going to recommend to the pastor that I be hired full time (one year contracts are the norm for the position.) Later we were to learn that the pastor made a statement which was just the opposite.

On April 15, I was to have N.W's funeral. The first shut-in who died on my watch was handled like this. As it became apparent that death was imminent, I told the man's wife that protocol demanded that I step aside and let the senior pastor take over. The widow to be agreed. The pastor made one or two calls on the patient before he died. When the patient passed, the senior pastor was asked to officiate at the funeral. Out of courtesy or whatever, he asked me to say a prayer which I did.

Now back to N.W.'s funeral. N.W. was dying. The pastor was in Michigan. I kept him posted by telephone. He came back two or three days before N.W. passed, but made no effort to call on him. When N.W. passed, his wife called me immediately. I told her that I would be there shortly. I called the pastor to see if he wanted to go with me. He did. We met at the church and rode together over to N.W.'s house. The corpse was still lying on the bed. I asked the pastor to pray over the body. We consoled the widow and then left.

Later the widow called me to make final arrangements. I said, "This is where senior pastor comes in." She said, "I do not want him, he doesn't even know N.W." I worried about the attitude the pastor would have about this, but went ahead with the funeral arrangements.

Since I was officiating, I thought I could make the order of the service. There was also another minister, his former pastor, who would have a part in the service.

I had pastor give the introduction and pray. When the service was over, we went to the cemetery for the interment. This was to be a military ceremony. As soon as the clergy part of the ceremony was over, I saw the pastor, out of the corner of my eye, leave the casket and go stand at the edge of the crowd gathered to mourn the deceased. I went ahead and completed the military part.

When I saw the pastor leave the casket and go to the edge of the crowd, I knew trouble was about to start. I had many clues that it was coming. We rode in silence back to the church and I went on with my duties. This was the beginning of rapid change with my relationship with the pastor.

April 20, I had a Board of Christian Life meeting. I had been on this board for about three years. During that time I had tried to bring about changes in the adult Sunday School curriculum with no success at all. At this meeting there was a proposal to bring in some outside consultants for some seminars. The chairman informed us that there would probably be cursing and swearing by these consultants. When the vote came down to have or not have these people, I was the only one to abstain. Everyone else voted in the affirmative to have them come.

By April 28, it was apparent to me that I was in deep trouble. By now I had observed that the pastor was not organized. He had little respect for the schedules of others and sometimes not even for his own. He would change the schedule of others at the drop of a hat, to accommodate his own needs or lack of planning. Because of this I was caught "out of sync" with several staff meeting changes in time.

Some staff members would roll their eyes and shrug their shoulders at me. This was of course, out of the sight of others.

I had observed some very subtle things taking place. My office was used as a storage room for unused trophies and broken furniture. Often I would come in and find boxes shoved up against my chair and desk. I would have to move them to get to my desk. I noticed that the music minister had a sign on his office which read "Music & Worship Interim." In contrast mine was left blank.

When I started to work I had quizzed the pastor about my appointment. I asked, "Will I be assigned an office?" The answer was "You will have L.D.'s old office next to mine." This turned out to be untrue. Two days later he assigned that office to his incoming youth pastor. I was assigned the office which you see pictured. Misrepresentation? I asked, "Will you announce my appointment?" The answer, "Yes, I will announce your appointment." He never did. This was also untrue. If it wasn't, what do you call it?

Top: Office of Interim Music Minister First Church
Bottom: My Office) Interim Visitation Pastor – left blank my whole tenure at First Church

Top: Inside My Office – Storage Materials First Church
Bottom: Broken Furniture, etc. in front of my desk at First Church

I noticed he was having the younger men open the morning worship services. He never asked me to do that. I noticed that he was using me to crowd the executive pastor away from Altar work on Sunday mornings. It became apparent to me that I was not being treated the same as the rest of the staff. He would say to me, "Is P.D. treating you all right?" One day he said, "Can I put you in the preaching schedule?" I told him that he could. I was scheduled to speak April 26 in the evening. I asked several friends to begin praying for me in that direction. There would be 5 days left in my contract at that point. Two or three days before I was to speak he called to cancel me. He said that "an itinerant semi-truck and trailer with a mission exhibit was coming through. They wanted to set up in our parking lot." And so I was canceled out. The Sunday Evening service started at 6:00 P.M. In my view it seemed that we could have had the regular evening service and then toured the mission exhibit trailer. He rebooked me for May 17 which would never be!

Somewhere shortly after the funeral of N.W. he started changing my contract. I was told that I wouldn't make hospital calls. If I did, he would tell me who I would call on and who I wouldn't call on. He began to marginalize my assignment. He did this by telling the two youth pastors to go and make calls on people that had been my assignments. Soon, I found myself being preempted on calls. I would go to a nursing home or hospital only to discover another pastor was there or had been there ahead of me. This was not only embarrassing, but a waste of the Lord's resources in my view.

Remember, this had been my church home for ten years. Two of my friends were in the hospital. The pastor informed me that I was not to call on them. Soon I received calls from two prominent board members inquiring about the health of my two friends. I said, "I can't tell you anything because pastor told me not to call on them." He said, "He would do that?" The board members said, "You go and call anyway, it is part of your job." In a later discussion with the pastor I pointed out what board members had said about this situation. The pastor said, "You don't work for the board, you work for me!"

On April 28 the pastor invited me to go with him to make a hospital call and then have lunch with him. We went and I was embarrassed because the prep room was so full of people that the nurses could hardly do their jobs.

After the call we went to a local restaurant for lunch. I tried to share some ideas about the calling ministry. It was of no avail. After some hurtful comments to me, pastor said, "If you want to be a pastor, why don't you go and apply to Dr. L?" The comment cut to the quick!

When we got back to the church I ran into the executive pastor in a hallway. He said, "Wayne, what is the matter, you are white as a sheet." I told him I had just been run over by a Mack truck!

On April 30 which was the last day of my first interim contract, I was available to call and sitting right in my office. The pastor claimed he had 5 surgeries and a funeral. He could not do hospital calls. This was the kind of situation I had tried to talk with him about previously.

Instead of sending me to do hospital calls, he left me sitting in my office and sent the executive pastor and others to make the hospital calls. In the afternoon I waited until the end of the day when he called me into his office and handed me another 90 day interim contract. A 6th grader could have written this contract in twenty minutes. All hospital work was deleted from this contract. Any calling of that type would be at the discretion of the pastor. I had expected a one year contract. Hadn't I proved myself yet? I felt like this contract was a vote of "no confidence." It was injurious to me. He summed it up by saying, "I have already interviewed four guys for this position." There was not a deadline for signing the contract so I walked out without signing it. I took a copy with me.

All the hurts of the past came over me like a flood! I called in the church secretary to my office. I told her I was resigning from all my duties with the church and might not come back to the Church of the Nazarene. If it happens it will be the end of 150 years of service to the Nazarenes spanning three generations. It was obvious to me that pastor had no intent to keep me.

On May 6, I received a phone call from a prominent board member. He told me, "not to hold my breath!" At first I thought this was supportive. Later events made me very uncertain that this was true.

On May 7, I had a visit from M.P. another board member. This person urged me to get the misunderstanding with the pastor straightened out.

So on May 8th, I met with pastor at Starbucks. I tried to straighten out any misunderstandings. I concluded afterward that the conversation went nowhere. My wife and I talked. We decided that we shouldn't let the conduct of a stranger drive us from our happy church home of ten years. We talked more that night and decided that I should sign the second interim contract and see where it played out. I signed the contract in front of my wife and called the pastor. I was told by pastor that he would see me Monday morning.

On Monday morning May 1, I called the church office to see what time the pastor would see me. I was informed that he was in a scheduled district meeting about a merger. It was obvious when he told me he would see me Monday morning that he already knew he had a scheduled meeting.

May 13, in a phone conversation with pastor, he ended up saying, "Don't come back emotions are running too high." Having suspected that this was going to be a total disaster, I had requested to be officially retired from the Church of the Nazarene. This was in process for the coming Assembly. The pastor did not know I had applied for retirement. Working after retirement was not an obstacle.

On May 20, the pastor ran mid-week prayer service himself. I had scheduled his new youth pastor to speak. It was also the night when the Verity Institute Choir would be there. The attendance that night was 130. I had worked hard with another couple to cultivate a relationship with the students from Verity. That night and in subsequent weeks the pastor would take credit for the work my wife and I had done. He had the bully pulpit and his bully newsletter. I could not defend myself in anyway.

Meanwhile my wife and I had decided that we would at least try to keep attending church there. She had always played for our Sunday School class.

On May 28 the pastor received a visit from S.J. on our behalf. S.J. and his wife supported me in the midweek service. They were informed by the pastor that a blank contract was laying on his desk waiting for me to sign. This was another untruth. He already knew

I had signed the contract and that he had told me not to come back. The contract on his desk was a duplicate of the one he gave me to sign.

Also, on May 28 we had S.P. and his wife at our home for games and fellowship. We also learned that the next morning on the 29th that S.P. was observed having breakfast with the pastor in a local restaurant. We also found out that on the evening of the 28th our son from Michigan had placed a call to K.K. Our son had gone on a mission trip with a group of people from First church. They had learned to love him very much. Our son knew we had a lot of friends at First Church so he called K.K. to see what was going on with his parents. He was told a story which was not accurate but had been put in circulation possibly by the pastor.

On May 29th we were just getting ready to go out to dinner when the telephone rang. It was the Rev. W.W. He was in a total rage. He called me a liar and said I was telling people that he had destroyed my ministry in Michigan years before. He claimed that someone had told him that.

I explained that I never said that. I further elaborated that I might have told a very, very few friends that he had destroyed the historical record of Christ Community written in stone. I said "I hear that you beat the monuments with sledge hammers!" He said, "I did not. I hooked them on my tractor and towed them out in back of the church." "I'm going to take your credentials." I said," I don't think you can touch me, the District Advisory Board has already processed my retirement!" I didn't know if he could defrock me or not. I said, "I am going to be in Michigan next week. I will take pictures and will see if you are telling me the truth." I then said, "This conversation needs to end because it is going nowhere." All of a sudden, like someone had shut off a spigot, he purred, "I will pray for you and Marilyn."

That same night I called my boy in Michigan. I asked if he would run up to what was now called Crossroads and take some pictures. Within 24 hours I had the pictures in my computer. The historical monument lay on its back in the field behind the church. My boy could not find a trace of the Nazarene monument. There was a sidewalk leading to a footing. The tree which we planted by the monument was still there.

The next week-end my boy and I searched the property. The vegetation was very heavy. The historic monument was laying on its back (pictures enclosed.) We found a broken pile of bricks from the original sign. Obviously, they were broken up with sledge hammers. Suddenly it dawned on us that there were tire tracks throughout the grass in all the little fields behind the church. My son said, "Dad these tracks were not here last Saturday!" Pictures are what we found in the summer of 2009.

Christ Community – Crossroads
2009 Cornerstones – Ebenezers gone

Top: 2009
Ruble at Crossroads - Christ Community

Bottom:
2009
Historical Monument Crossroad - Christ Community

Top: 2009
Backside Crossroads – Christ Community

Bottom: 2009
Former site of the Bridge Builders Memorial
Crossroads – Christ Community

2009
Crossroads – Christ Community Historical Monument

Someone had been searching for the Nazarene monument. They didn't find it! Either the Rev. W.W. was up here this week working with his house or he sent a friend. Can you imagine the outcry if President Obama had the Viet Nam Memorial bulldozed down! So I have been told an untruth again!

On May 30th a church member and the staunchest friend a person ever could have paid a visit to the pastor. This person took a witness. The pastor first pointed out that he didn't want the midweek to be an alternate service. This person told the pastor that they wanted me back. His reply was that I had been given a contract and refused to sign it. My friend told him this was not true, that I had signed the contract. The pastor then came back with the fact that he had polled 4 board members and they told him (the pastor) that emotions were running too high and it would be best if I didn't come back.

The pastor suggested that the 4 board members all knew me. These included R.J. My friend was shocked because she knew that R.J. was one of our friends. The pastor claimed that at a breakfast with myself I presented him with a contract to do both prayer meeting and visitation. This was a twisted half-truth. The pastor had sketched his plans for the future which included him earning his doctoral degree. This would result in a narrowing of the time he could put in on the pastorate. I told him what I had done in a similar situation. I had hired an associate. I suggested that about 4 years earlier I had been given a model contract offer by First Church which included visitation and prayer meeting. He asked to see this contract.

Subsequently, I provided W.W. a copy of what the offer of four years ago entailed. I guess this became the basis of a new 90 day interim contract. The remuneration was based on what the church offered me four years ago.

Next the pastor started to do a real hatchet job on myself. He claimed that Dr. T.L. and Dr. S.A. had advised him not to give me a permanent contract. He added that we had problems in Michigan and everywhere we had been. He reiterated that Dr. T.L. had told him not to bring Wayne Greve back to prayer meeting.

The conversation then shifted to what I had accomplished as calling pastor. My friend told him about a call I made to them as visitation pastor. They had grumbled about the music. I had defended pastor W.W. I then had prayer and left. The pastor then faulted me about hospital calls I had made. The accusation was distorted and untrue!

The conversation ranged on about soccer and evangelism. The pastor had scheduled a revival, but decided to combine it with Faith Promise which is a missionary event. He booked his former D.S. to be the speaker. This is a prime example of what goes on in the Church of the Nazarene.

On June 7 of 2001, we worshiped at Flint Central. We saw the same style worship service that the Rev. W.W. had implemented at First Church in Indianapolis.

In the meantime my wife and I had talked the situation over. We concluded that First Church had been mostly our happy home for ten years. Why should we let a newcomer drive us away, even if he was the pastor? The first Sunday back we tried hard. Marilyn played for Sunday school like she always did. After she was done playing she said, "Honey, I don't think I can do this!" We could sense people politely withdrawing from us. Then in the corridors it started. We would run into someone we knew and M.J. would burst into tears. M.J. said, "I don't have control over this – it just happens."

S.P. had contacted me to see if I would eat breakfast with him. I agreed, so we met at the Bob Evans restaurant on Shadeland Avenue at 10:00 a.m. on June 17, 2009. I asked him point-blank if in the ten years we had known him, if we had ever caused trouble. He said, "No!"

I asked him if he had heard that we were trouble-makers before we got to First Church. He dropped his head and said, "No!" I believe he perjured himself. He has not called us for two weeks since he met with the pastor.

We tried one more Sunday to worship at First Church. My wife broke into tears almost as soon as she crossed the threshold. As soon as she would see one of our close friends she would break into sobs. This happened with one of my wife's close friends. And the lady retracted like M.J. had leprosy! In the weeks ahead I would find out our situation.

The psalmist described it well in the 31st Psalm. "Because of all my adversaries I have become a reproach, but especially among my neighbors, and a dread to my friends! Those from outside who saw me fled from me. I am forgotten as a dead man, out of mind; I am like a broken vessel."

"For I have heard the whispering slander of many; terror is on every side; they plotted together against me, they planned to take away my life." (work)

"But I trusted in you O Lord"; I said, "You are my God."

"My times are in your hand: deliver me from the hand of my enemies, and from those who persecute me."[15]

My wife would cry herself to sleep for weeks. Never did my D.S. and wife ever contact us. They brought down the ice-age on our heads! We wondered what happened to compassion, holiness and all the other traits that they espoused and preached about.

On the same day I met with S.P., I also met with R.J. He wanted me to tell him everything that had happened. I did! Then I showed him pictures of the destruction at Christ Community which happened around 2001 and 2002. R.J. seemed very upset about his name being in the sworn affidavit. I tried to get him to focus on us, but it was hard! R.J. finally suggested three courses of action for us. (1) Sue the pastor and incur the wrath and hate of the Church of the Nazarene. (2) Bring in an arbitrator (Dr. T.L., D.S.) and meet pastor W.W. and go over everything blow by blow. My comment was "Dr. T.L. would not be neutral!" (3) Leave the church and the Nazarenes and just go away quietly. Get lost! I told R.J. that another board member wanted to talk with me the next week. R.J. did not want me to meet with this individual. I don't know why!

I suggested that none of the options were very palatable. The least hurtful for all involved would be for us to take option 3.

Although extremely painful, it seemed best to adopt option three. On June 21, 2009 we left First Church behind us with great sadness. For now we are leaving our membership there in hope that someday we might be able to come back!

These were my thoughts as we left: "Today we broke from our church home of ten years. This may be the break from our denomination! Through three generations our family has served this denomination. This covers a span of about 150 years. During my Father-in-law's last ten or fifteen years of life he made an agreement with God that he would give a million dollars to the Church of the Nazarene if God would spare his life for fifteen years.. Three generations of our family have attended this local church." After Mother's death the day after 9-11, we knew what mother wished. We children knew our personal needs too. But Mother wanted us to give $50,000 to the Bible College in Colorado Springs. My wife was the executrix for her Mother's estate. We talked some more and decided it was the right thing to do. Two from my wife's family and I traveled to Colorado Springs and made the presentation. None of this seemed to matter now. Our honesty, faith, integrity and hard work were nothing. We had gotten in the way of a First Church pastor and D.S., therefore, we were trash!

When a first church pastor poisons most of your friends and your reputation behind the scenes, you are expected to just fade away! This is a First Church! Don't rock the boat! The D.S. begins Operation Deep Freeze. You begin to feel the freeze everywhere! Only a very few, very strong friends stick with you. They pay a price!

Yes, today we are all alone as we look for a new church home, new friends and new relationships. As Coleridge said, "Alone, alone, all, all alone. Alone on a wide, wide sea and never a saint took pity on our souls in agony."[16]

This is the parable of the Good Samaritan all over again as the great host of our friends pass by us on the other side of the road.

My wife has sobbed herself to sleep for months. I have had sleepless mornings since our lives caved in. I awake at about 3:00 a.m and reiterate in my mind all the things that have happened to us. I have very bad dreams when I do sleep. Last night it was Yellow Jackets stinging me from head to foot.

We wonder where is our D.S? Isn't he supposed to be pastor of pastors? Where is his wife? Doesn't she ever comfort pastor's wives? No, all we get is the ice age. Total shunning! We wondered what happened to compassion, holiness and all the traits that they espoused and preached.

Strange thoughts race through my mind. What about all those wonderful people in nursing homes, hospitals, and shut-ins? They have no clue what happened to us. Some keep asking, but I cannot tell! My ministry is like chopped off at the knees!

In Psalm 5:12-14 the Bible describes my situation. "For it is not an enemy who reviled me – then I could have borne it. It is not one who hates me who magnified himself against me – or I would hide myself from him.

But it is you, a man of my equal, my guide and my acquaintance.

We took sweet counsel together and walked into the house of God in company.[17]

The Psalmist further describes my senior pastor. Psalm 55:21 says, "The words of his mouth were smoother than butter, but war was in his heart; his words were softer than oil, yet they were drawn swords."[18]

Behind the scenes the Rev. W.W. was full of calumny and trickery. To deceive or confuse were in his heart. Through false and malicious statements, he muddied our reputation. He did this with others too.

Around June 24, 2009 I learned that another, C.J. had been appointed to serve in the position I had held as interim. This gentleman came down from Michigan to Indiana at the same time as the Rev. W.W. He was also connected with W.W's past. He was in a church on the Indianapolis district for one year. The church had seemingly split under his ministry.

The objectives of the "prince" at this moment are more or less completed as regards to staffing First Church. It has culminated in what I call the Acorn Configuration. The Acorn Configuration not only shows the cronyism that exists in the Church of the Nazarene, but it shows the nepotism that is practiced without a blush!

Topsy Turvy in The Church of the Nazarene

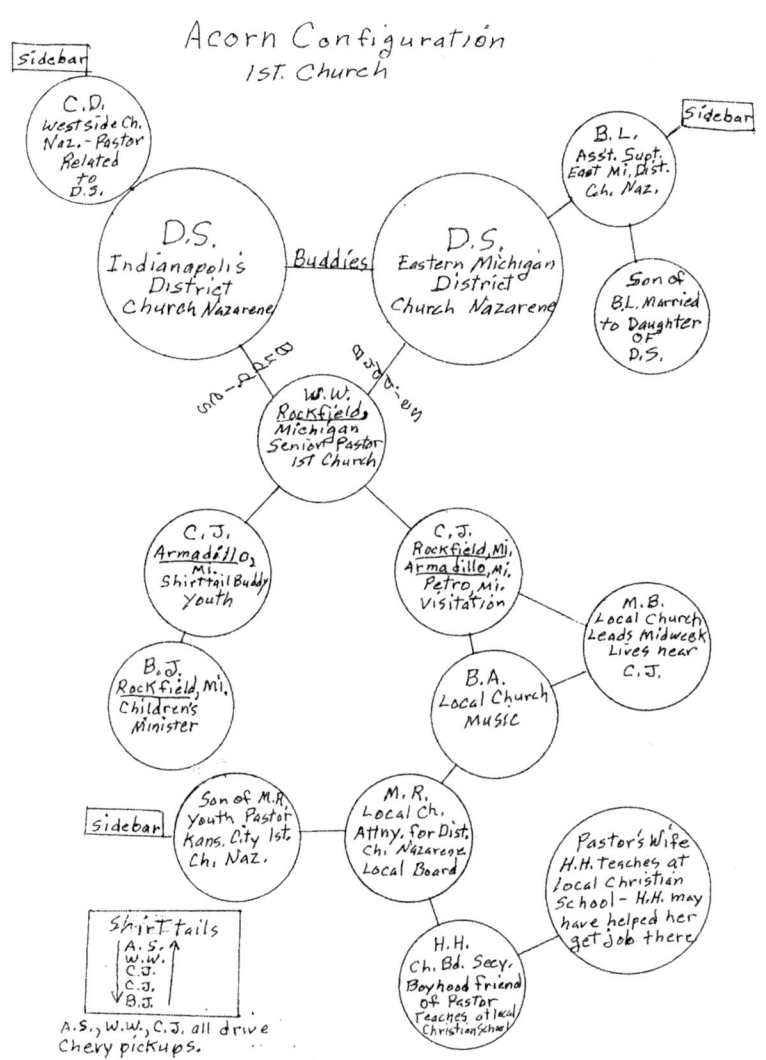

Acorn Configuration
First Church
Indianapolis

On June 30, 2009 I met with H.G., a board member, for breakfast at Bob Evans. The meeting was cordial. He mentioned that he had a pact with another board member that if either ever left the church, the other one would leave too.

On July 9, 2009 I met S.P. the second time for breakfast. This time he admitted that he and the pastor had talked about me. He never did say what it was about and I did not press him to tell me.

In the cases of the executive pastor and the children's minister here is what happened. The "prince" pulled in the entire board on this one. The couples were not given 30 days notice, (a manual requirement.) They were given 15 days notice. Each party was forced to write a resignation. To cover their departure they were given what could be called severance pay in the public workplace. They were told that if they made one squeak about their departure the pastor had the option to cut their severance pay. To me, this smacks of legal blackmail and runs against all Christian principles I know anything about!

In order to bring the latter off the "prince" needed reasons for his actions. I am not sure what he told the board. I know what he told me! He used two items against B.Z. in my presence. First, he said she was not 100% loyal to the "prince" Secondly, he said, "Have you heard the story about N. & B.Z?" I told him that I did not want to hear the story.

In the case of the executive pastor, W.W. first hit me with "How do I get rid of P.D.?" Secondly, "P.D. is too expensive!" thirdly, "P.D. is not needed around here!" We read in the Bible, Acts 7:58 "And cast him out of the city and stoned him. And the witnesses laid down their garments at the feet of a young man named Saul."[19] And, in chapter 8:1 "Now Saul had consented to killing him." (Stephen)[20] Saul was as guilty of killing Stephen as those who threw the rocks. The First Church board was as guilty of the figurative deaths of the executive pastor and the children's minister as was the "prince."

As I tell this, the youth pastor saw what was happening to himself and he got busy and got a job in another state and got out of there! The "prince" now has it all his way with staffing.

Now let's examine how the "prince" functions. First, the Prince injures only the people from whom he takes away positions. He gives their positions to newcomers. These people form a small minority of the whole congregation and are forced to leave. They can never become dangerous." All others being left unmolested, are in consequence easily quieted, and at the same time are afraid to make a false move, lest they share the fate of those who have been deprived of their possessions (positions)."[21]

This "prince" leaves a trail of innocent victims. They remain poor and scattered. The main congregations are pandered to and exploited. Almost all our friends abandoned us. These are people who have known us for ten years.

Secondly, there is the question of loyalty. This (minister) prince must create ways to make his staff and congregation loyal to him. He must be an authority figure that they can always depend on. "Wherefore, a wise prince (minister) should devise means whereby his subjects may at all times, whether favourable or adverse, feel the need of the State (church)and of him, for then they will always be faithful to him."[22] Yes, this "prince" demands 100% loyalty to himself. Loyalty to the Lord is secondary!

Thirdly, the (minister) Prince who wants to maintain control must discard virtue." It is essential, therefore, for a Prince who would maintain his position, to have learned to be other than good, and to use or not to use his goodness as necessity requires."[23] For this "prince" the latter includes deceit, misrepresentation, manipulating people and any kind of intrigue to get where he wants to go.

Fourthly, "A prince (minister) should therefore disregard the reproach of cruelty where it enables him to keep his subjects united and faithful."[24] The end justifies the means even if you sacrifice honesty, fairness and other virtues. So he wipes out the staff and selects his own team. Meantime he panders to his congregation in many ways. "What a great church this is!" He uses funerals to build prestige with his congregation.

Fifthly, "And here comes the question whether it is better to be loved rather than feared, or feared rather than loved. It might be answered that we should wish to be both; but since love and fear can hardly coexist together, if we must choose between them, it is far better to be feared than loved."[25] This prince measures up to these criteria. He wants all his staff ensconced around his own office so he can keep an eye on them. He micro manages every one of them. Therefore, he keeps the fear in them at all times.

Sixthly, A prince (minister) should understand how to use well both the man and the beast."[26] If he doesn't he can't survive. Yes, this prince can play the part of both beast and man. He can be furious and then flip a coin and purr like a kitten.

Seventhly, ". . . a prudent Prince (minister) neither can nor ought to keep his word when to keep it is hurtful to him and the causes which led him to pledge it are removed."[27] So it is fine for the "prince" to make promises he has no intention of keeping. After all, he and he alone, decides if the reasons for which he made the promise no longer exist!

Eighthly, ". . . no Prince was ever at a loss for plausible reasons to cloak a breach of faith. It is necessary indeed, to put a good colour on this nature, and to be skilful in feigning and dissembling. But men are so simple, and governed so absolutely by their present needs, that he who wishes to deceive will never fail in finding willing dupes."[28] This "prince" is always planning ahead with excuses for his actions.

Lastly, "A Prince (minister) should therefore be very careful that nothing ever escapes his lip which is not replete with the five qualities above named, so that to see and hear him, one would think him the embodiment of mercy, good faith, integrity, kindliness, and religion. And here I know no virtue which it is more necessary for him to possess than this last; because men in general judge rather by the eye than by the hand, for all can see but few can touch. Every one sees what you seem, but few know what you are, and these few dare not expose themselves to the opinion of the many who have the majesty of the State (church) to back them up."[29]

Does this "prince" have these latter qualities? Yes, he has them. He can appear to be a kind and religious man while planning to do you in. He can appear to the congregation to be kind and religious while he is busy "doing in" the minority. The mass of the congregation sees him as he appears to be. He slaughters anyone who he thinks is getting in his way.

Let's put in juxtaposition what Machiavelli's philosophy is with that of Biblical writers. Let's start with the <u>Lost Books of the Bible</u>. Hermes III Commands says, "Moreover he said unto me, love truth;

and let all the speech be true which proceeds out of thy mouth." "They therefore that lie, deny the Lord, and become robbers of the Lord, not rendering to God what they received from Him. For they received the spirit free from lying: If therefore they make that a liar, they defile what was committed to them by the Lord, and become deceivers."[30]

Now let's move to the Canonized Bible. In <u>Ephesians</u> 4 and 5 we find instructions for the sanctified. 4:24 ". . . Put on the new man,"4:25 ". . . Put away lies and speak the truth. . . " 4:31 "Let all bitterness, and indignation and wrath, and clamor, and evil speaking be removed from you . . . " 5:6 "Do not let anyone deceive you with vain words; . . ." Again, instructions are given for the righteous: 5:7 "<u>Do not be joint partakers with them.</u>" 5:11 "And have no fellowship with the unfruitful works of darkness, <u>but rather expose them</u>."[31] The Bible seems to teach that it is our Christian duty to expose those who deceive.

Perhaps Colossians succinctly sums it up with these words: 3:9 "Do not lie to one another . . ."[32] In Ephesians, Galatians, and Colossians traits are listed which seem to be possessed by the "prince." It is certainly apparent that these traits are not endorsed by the Bible. In fact, hatred, jealousy, contentions, divisions, envying and social cliques for personal gain are condemned in the Bible.

On October 17, 2009 I conducted interviews with some of the minority victims left behind by the "prince." I must be very careful of their identities. These interviewees held positions under the "prince."

The first interviewee said, "W.W. divides people by pitting one against another. Lies are commonplace, He gets you to tell two or three negative things about yourself and then turns around and uses them against you to force you out of your position." He is totally deceptive. He destroys people whom he perceives are in his way to achieve his personal goals. He can be very smooth in his manipulations. He leaves a trail of broken people behind him. Many are lost to the church and others are lost to God." This compares to the author of "<u>Don't Call Me Brother.</u>"[33] "He took our church from over 900 to just a few over 500 in attendance." These interviewees concluded "that W.W. is either psychotic or very sinful or a combination of both!" Another interviewee had a harrowing experience before being forced out. He, and another associate were given loans by the church as a down payment on their homes. The agreement was that for every year they worked their loans would be reduced by $1,000. They both left. One individual's loan was forgiven. The other person had a lien slapped on his home by the church. He had to borrow from his relatives to pay the lien off so he could sell his home. This all happened under the watch of W.W. I have tried to find an explanation for the kinds of behavior the "prince" has exhibited in this chapter. For instance, professional books in discussions about liars list these kinds: <u>Consumate</u> – great skill, <u>Inveterate</u> - a deep rooted habit, <u>Psychopathic</u> - has an irresistible compulsion to lie – often for no rational or sane reason (example), "I won 3,000 Nazarenes to the Eastern Michigan District." <u>Unconscionable</u> - lack of regret or remorse, <u>Egregious</u> – viciousness of his lies.

Some other sources discuss these definitions: <u>Pathological Liar</u> – abnormal variation from a sound or proper condition. Governed by compulsion, <u>Egomaniac</u> – abnormally excessive egotism, <u>Abuse</u> – mistreating, <u>Sadism</u> – the getting of pleasure from inflicting physical or psychological pain on another or others, <u>Misrepresent</u> – to represent falsely: give an untrue or misleading idea. The latter seem to reflect behavior characteristics of our "prince."

I have tried to figure out how the conduct of the "prince" squares with the teachings of the Church of the Nazarene. There is no match. I have been told that on October 25, 2009 W.W. preached a short sermon about lying, deceit, and manipulation. The spirit that exists within him accuses others of the very things he is guilty of himself! Prior to this, in the month of October the D.S. came to First Church to hold a "one day revival." In the evening he spent about 15 minutes of his sermon defending W.W. This is after W.W. had pastored First Church for over a year. I wondered why the D.S. needed to do that!

What I share in this chapter is shared on behalf of the <u>minority</u>. There is a trail of brokenness left behind by the "prince." Other ministers have corroborated this with me. I cannot find anything in the Bible which supports these kinds of actions on the part of a pastor. Why do I share these kinds of behind the scenes activities in the

Church of the Nazarene? Because reading this might start reform in the church! My only hope is that they might re-examine themselves and open their hearts to a genuine revival which leads them back to their early beginnings! As for forgiveness, we forgive one and all!

"The expulsion of Roberts and his followers from the Methodist Episcopal Church <u>laid bare the nearly limitless power of the nineteenth century bishops.</u>"
Jones, C. E., <u>Perfectionist Persuasion</u>, *(The Scarecrow Press, Inc., 1974) P. 10.*

Chapter Eleven

Ironclad Power

District Superintendents in the Church of the Nazarene have almost unlimited power. One could say that they are popish in their power. They can make travel destinations that may be at various points around the world or in the continental United States. They usually make six figures in salaries and benefits. At various points I will describe two districts which are similar in power and scope.

This Comparison is on District Superintendents

Indianapolis District Superintendent 2008

Salary & Benefits	$129,157
Parsonage Utilities	13,291
Auto	17,404
Professional Expenses	3,731
Total	$163,583

Misc., gifts, revivals, access to other funds – unknown[34]

2007

Salary, Benefits, Taxes	$130,429
Parsonage, Utilities	16,373
Auto	15,073
Professional Expenses	23,731
Total	$185,606

Revivals, gifts, etc are unknown, but extras[36]

Eastern Michigan District Superintendent 2009

Annuity	$20,000
Health/Life Insurance	15,693
Housing Allowance	36,000
Social Security	15,000
Medical Reimbursement	500
Cash Salary	56,038
Prof. Reimbursement	14,000
Auto Reimbursement	15,000
Total	$172,231

Misc. would include Revivals, gifts, postage, Love offerings, communications. Unknown beyond salary and benefits. Although it looks like a $2,000 cut in pay from 2008 to 2009, he actually got a $5,000 increase in his annuity[35]

2008

Annuity	$15,000
Health/Life Insurance	12,471
Housing Allowance	36,000
Medical Reimbursement	500
Social Security	15,000
Cash Salary	58,088
Prof. Reimbursement	14,000
Auto Reimbursement	15,000
Total	$166.059

Adds are revivals, love offerings, etc.[37]

2006
Salary & Benefits $131,951
Parsonage & Utilities 13,478
Auto 10,943
Professional 24,052
Total $180,424

Revivals, love offerings & gifts are unknown, but above and beyond total.[38]

2005
Salary & Benefits $121,594
Parsonage & Utilities 13,177
Auto 12,646
Prof. Reimbursement 26,109
Total $173,526

Revivals, love offering & gifts are unknown, but above and beyond total.[40]

2004
Salary & Benefits $123,653
Parsonage & Utilities 22,114
Auto 13,008
Professional 16,134
Total $174,909

Add to total revivals, gifts. etc.[42]

2007
Annuity $18,750
Health/Life Insurance 13,084
Housing Allowance 36,000
Medical Reimbursement 1,497
Social Security 14,501
Prof. Reimbursement 14,000
Auto Reimbursement 15,000
Cash Salary 57,276
Total $170,108

Add onns are revivals, love offering, etc. above and beyond total.[39]

2006
Annuity $15,000
Health/Life Insurance 12,553
Housing Allowance 36,000
Medical Reimbursement 1,199
Social Security 14,000
Cash Salary 59,060
Prof. Reimbursement 10,000
Auto Reimbursement 15,000
Total $162,812

Adds are: revivals, love offerings, postage, Christmas Bonus, etc.[41]

2005
Annuity $11,250
Health/Life Insurance 9,129
Housing Allowance 27,000
Medical Reimbursement 975
Social Security 10,500
Cash Salary 43,372
Prof. Reimbursement 6,300
Auto Reimbursement 10,350
Total $118,876

Adds are revivals, love offering, etc.[43]

2003		2004	
Salary & Benefits	$57,600	Annuity	$10,500
Annuity	7,552	Health/Life Insurance	11,943
Disability Insurance	2,906	Housing Allowance	36,000
Health Insurance	11,299	Medical Benefits	2,500
Medical Reimbursement	4,326	Social Security	14,000
Taxes		Cash Salary	56,818
State	3,117	Prof. Reimbursement	9,600
Federal	6,748	Auto Reimbursement	13,800
Social Security	13,714	Total	$155,161
Christmas Gift	1,450		
Vacation Bonus	1,450	Adds would be revivals, love offerings and other funds he has access to.[45]	
Auto	12,460		
Housing	21,682		
Prof. Reimbursement	11,784		
Total	$156,088		

Adds were revivals and etc.[44]

So, one can see that District Superintendents are reimbursed handsomely. In terms of remuneration they are probably on a par with their counterparts in the secular world. They may even be overcompensated for the work they do!

District Superintendents practically have unlimited power to place ministers in churches. This is how it works. The District Superintendent can come to a typical church board and say, "I have three pastoral recommendations for your church." The Board will say "But of these three which one do you recommend?" This is the Superintendent's golden moment to put in a friend or relative or someone who has "buttered him up."

If the superintendent doesn't paint a pretty enough picture of his candidate, or it is a strong church board and they reject his first pick, then he can go to another first choice he may have waiting in the wings.

If a pastor gets placed primarily through the influence of a District Superintendent, then he is eternally in bondage to that superintendent. The pastor must forever be a "yes man" to whatever course the superintendent pursues. He is forever caught in the power web the superintendent weaves. If a typical pastor happens to get caught in the crosshairs of someone who is maybe better "connected," then he may discover that all his friends rapidly desert him. "Why?" They immediately begin asking themselves, "How will it affect me?"

Typical District Superintendents trade ministers between districts like slave masters. "Horse Trading" is common. "This guy is in trouble here, do you have a place on your district that I could put him?" And so, on and on it goes!

As a pastor, the D.S. can make or break you. You will see how this works as I tell about ironclad power in the next few paragraphs.

There is no doubt; District Superintendents in the Church of the Nazarene are very powerful. Some accrue more power than others. For instance, the District Superintendent of the Indianapolis District is the Chairman of the Regional College Board, he is a member of the General Board, member of the Publishing House Board and serves on other boards or strategic committees as necessity arises. These are powerful boards in the Church of the Nazarene. Also, he is a second generation D.S. He is also in a position to see that certain people are granted honorary doctorates from the regional college.

The District Superintendent is a slave driver for budgets and allocations. According to Nazarene periodicals 70% of all continental U.S. churches are less than one hundred. Many ministers in this range are whipped verbally, in print and otherwise. Their churches are embarrassed and they are embarrassed. The sun rises and sets on the budget or allocation. Success in ministry hinges on the budget or allocations.

The following excerpts are from D.S. reports from the Indianapolis District. 2000 "Churches have struggled for years to pay their allocations". 2002 Fair share allocation is 96% paid. I expect every church on the Indianapolis District, regardless of size and situation, to pay all your allocations in full." 2004 "District fair share paid 94%. Several churches didn't pay theirs because they did not plan. <u>Pastors who didn't pay must write a written plan and present it to the District Superintendent and the District Advisory Board</u>. This is the year of encouragement!"

2006 "Several churches could not pay their 14% allocation. <u>If they didn't achieve it they were asked to pay it weekly. All churches who</u>

failed must meet with the D.S., the District Finance Committee, the Secretary and the District Accountant to set up a weekly plan." 2007 "The 13 churches who didn't meet their allocations must send it in by the week. Every church must pay their allocations in full."[46]

The following excerpts are from the District Superintendent's reports on the Eastern Michigan District. 2002 "51 churches paid budget in full." 2006 "Commendation to 51 churches who paid budget in full. I plan to meet with every church board that did not pay their budget in full. The District goal among others is to pay the ministry budget in full." 2007 "54 churches paid their budget in full." 2008 "49 churches paid budget in full." 2009 "39 churches paid their budget in full."[47]

As one can see, budgets or allocations are a constant theme in the District Superintendent's reports. To succeed in ministry you need wonderful skills in the area of fund raising. In spite of intense pressure on pastors and churches, the budgets started to tumble on the Eastern Michigan District.

At the first sign of having accrued the displeasure of the D.S., the process of shunning begins. To say that this is a cruel treatment of humanity is an understatement! It is particularly cruel when one considers the doctrine that is taught by the Church of the Nazarene.

As soon as it was apparent that I had incurred the wrath of the "prince," the ice age began! First, we noticed that most of our friends at First Church began to pull away from us. People on the church board whom we thought were our friends dropped us immediately. Some would not even answer our letters. The church staff that I had amiable relationships with began to distance themselves from us. Of course, they had to work for the "prince!"

The D.S. and wife immediately put the deep freeze on our relationship. For several years he had invited us to sit at what he called "The table of his special friends." This had taken place at the annual 'pastors' Christmas Banquet. Supposedly, he was our friend because he had been a friend of my wife's Dad.

It now becomes apparent that the real reason was probably to extract a large gift from us for the district. I noted that several of the people at this table were heavy givers to the district and to the "pet" programs of the D.S.

How could it be that in one year we now have no invitation to the "special table" at the Christmas Banquet? Not only has this happened, but First Church which is supposed to pay the cost to the Christmas Banquet for all retired ministers in their membership has not even extended an invitation for us to attend the banquet!

At the 2009 Assembly retirement ceremony the wife of the D.S. would meet me in the aisle of the tabernacle and ungraciously say, "I suppose you are not speaking to us?" I would reply, "Yes, we are still speaking to you." This was the last time we would hear from either of them up to the point that I am telling this.

At the same retirement service the General Superintendent's wife and the wife of the District Superintendent were sitting directly in front of my wife and me. I tried to help the General's wife adjust her chair. She snapped at me that I wasn't doing it right. Now in all fairness she didn't know that in a few minutes her husband would be retiring me! On second thought, maybe she did know!

When M.L. was still pastor at First Church and things were rather turbulent, I had written a letter of concern to the Board of General Superintendents. Others had written too. The D.S. asked me if he could have a copy of the letter I had written. I dutifully gave him a copy. In short, I tried to do everything I knew how to do to support his leadership. It was to be of no avail!

The Lees greeting us at the Dedication of our New Home.

We even had him come with a number of our friends and dedicate our new home when we moved into it. Still at the slightest sign of conflict between me and his anointed for First Church, Ironclad Power kicked in. We were instant trash!

Our long years of labor, love, integrity and hard work for the Church of the Nazarene meant nothing. I guess we will never know what we did wrong. Honoring God's word, having integrity while under fire meant nothing. The placing of the "prince" at First Church was a result more of two D.S.s working in tandem with their buddy than it was on the part of the Lord.

We were supposed to sit under the ministry of a person who did not ring true to scripture. A person who could destroy other people at will with the blessing of two superintendents. This person was placed in strategic pulpits in the Church of the Nazarene by two scheming District Superintendents when they both knew he was problematic!

First Church pastors probably have ironclad power next to district superintendents. If it is apparent that they have the "blessing" of the D.S., they can pretty well tell their boards what they are going to do.

One very significant way for the "blessing" to be apparent is for the D.S. to call on a pastor to lead the prayer at a very significant convocation. In the Church of the Nazarene one of those very significant convocations is called Camp Meeting. At the 2009 Camp Meeting at Indianapolis this happened. For the last service of the Camp Meeting the D.S. brought in the First Church choir to sing. He then called on the First Church pastor to lead in prayer, thus giving him his highest approbation. The exact same thing happened in 2010. Yes, the "prince" got high visibility because the D.S. called on him in a high visibility situation.

The D.S. who called on the First Church pastor to pray at Camp Meeting was just as guilty of the unholy behavior of that said pastor as if he had behaved in the same way. Here goes Saul again! He didn't kill Stephen, but he held the clothes of those who did. Thus, he was just as guilty as those who threw the stones. Now I know that I will be condemned by the Church of the Nazarene for saying this, but truth is truth! When Stephen spoke the truth, his accusers gnashed their teeth because they were so angry.

At this time, 2009, it also became public knowledge that the Indianapolis District superintendent was one of the Camp Meeting speakers at the Eastern Michigan Camp Meeting. The youth pastor at First Church was also the youth speaker at the Eastern Michigan Camp Meeting. The "prince" was also there. It is not known if he was there in an official capacity. He did claim at First Church that he went up to Michigan to take care of his Mother.

As a newcomer to the Indianapolis District the "prince" was also placed on a high visibility committee. This created much dissatisfaction among other ministers on the district who had much more tenure. This committee was studying the merger of two districts. W.W. also functions on a committee at the regional university, so again we have ironclad power.

In about 2005 I tried to find out my pastor's salary and benefits. The following information was as close as I could get. This information is from the district minutes.

District Minutes
2005 - First Church
Column 16
Pastor's Actual Cash Salary
$66,725
All pastors are lumped together so no one knows what each pastor is getting for housing.
Column 10
Health & Hospital Exclusion Allowance
$60,885
Again, all pastors and employees are lumped together so no one can figure what each is getting.
Column 5A
Local Church Expenses Reimbursements
$42,025
Again, pastors and staff are lumped together so no one can figure out what each one is getting.
What is Clear?

Column 3A
{Pastor's Cash Salary
$45,105
Column 3B
Pastor's Employee Benefits
$27,106
Annuity, Life Insurance, Social Security
Total $72,211.00
Plus
Auto, Housing, Revivals, Gifts and Utilities. [48]

Shouldn't it be public knowledge to Church Members what they are paying their pastor in cash and benefits? I am guessing that salary and benefits approaches $100,000. It appears that there is no way to determine the actual salary and benefits of the pastor at First Church. It is a secret known only to the few!

So with the money comes the power. The "prince" has the power of money, prestige, influence, the bully pulpit and the weekly newsletter. He can also "swing" the church board anyway he wants to go. He can slant his pulpit and his newsletter any way he wants to take them. What about me? I am the minority, helpless victim. They just want me to go away and shut up! What chance do I have to state or tell what has happened to me? What can I do against a triangle of power that seems invincible? If it hasn't happened to the main congregation, they won't believe a word I say. No, not even if I am an honest man!

It's also worth saying right here that first churches have different standards than small ones. Of course their standards are unwritten, but they are operant nonetheless.

What comes to my mind at this moment is a verse in John 15:13 "No one has greater love than this, that one lay down his life (ego and power - my paraphrase) for his friends."[49] Now if I was a real friend wouldn't the D.S. at least try to arbitrate my situation? Wouldn't he be concerned about salvaging the situation? Wouldn't he be touched by the human sorrow of my wife and me? No, nothing but the ice age! He has learned well the lessons from his former boss at the regional college. He has learned how to be insensitive and uncaring. All this in the face of what he said in his report of 2003. He referred to William Barclay vol.2 of the Daily Study Bible. He said, "Barclay deals with 'profession without practice' and explains that it is condemned."

He then refers to David McKenna's book, <u>Wesleyan leadership In Troubled Times</u>. McKenna deals with profession without practice. He, the D.S., concludes by saying, "Never maintain profession without practice."[50] It seems like you can utter these platitudes in the Church of the Nazarene, but leaders never have to live up to them! Yes, ironclad power seems to corrupt! It seems to destroy. We are a part of the voiceless history of the Church of the Nazarene!

"History repeats itself."   Unknown

Chapter Twelve

Crossroads Collapses, 2009

In 2002, Dr. S.A. made a presentation to the District Assembly. He presented Dundee and Crossroads as being newly organized churches. No one seems to know where the people came from to start Crossroads or where they disappeared to when W.W. suddenly left. Some thought they were relatives and friends of W.W. The minutes do indicate that some of the church officers were from the Davison area. This was where W.W. lived at the time.

What is strange is that in the minutes of 2002, W.W. reported no members and only Sunday morning attendance and Sunday School attendance. One wonders how you could organize a church with no members!

At the same assembly W.W. would expound on the wonders of starting a "new church." Namely, Crossroads. It took over eight years of hard labor and prayers to give birth to Christ Community. It lasted 20 years and then it crashed because of a pastor.

In its next life someone would spend about a year destroying all monuments, signs, crosses and cornerstones. The chapel would be gutted and made into a playpen. The kitchen and fellowship hall would be partitioned. What I had heard was supposed to be a gym had become the sanctuary with portable chairs for pews. Now when you come in the front entrance you are faced with a playpen. Then you go through a partitioned area and then you arrive at the worship area. Crossroads would last 7 years and then crash under S.R.

In interviewing people who attended there, they told me that Dr. S.A. had been told that the minister was adrift. Perhaps doctrinally. The D.S. did nothing so they left.

In chapter 13 of Matthew, Jesus told the parable of the Sower. It describes what happened to some of the seed. Verse 5 says, "Some fell upon the rocky places, where they had not much soil; and immediately they sprang up because the soil was not deep enough." verse 6, "But after the sun rose, they were scorched; and because they did not have roots, they dried up."[51]

Later in the chapter Jesus explains the parable. This is what he says about the stony ground. Verse 20-21 "Now the one who was sown upon the rocky places is the one who hears the word and immediately receives it with joy. But because he has no root in himself, he does not endure; for when tribulation or persecution arises because of the word he is quickly offended."[52] Perhaps this parable explains why the church mushroomed in attendance for one year under W.W. and then began to recede and vanish away when he left. Perhaps they were more attached to the messenger than to the Lord of the Bible.

In 2004, the D.S. would characterize W.W. as "one of the leading church planting experts in the denomination." Yet, five years later many of the new starts on the Eastern Michigan District would be dead, including Crossroads.

At the time of the New Start Crossroads I would receive glowing reports from both D.S's about how great it was doing. To date I have had a difficult time getting information out of anyone who knows about the physical destruction which took place on the property. They either prevaricate to me or refuse to tell me what they know. I just search for truth. My search for truth continues.

I do know that the seven years Crossroads remained open presents a suspect history. In 2002, W.W. reported an average of 126 in morning worship with no members. In 2003, S.R. reported 6 members. In 2004 S.R.. reported 47 members I am guessing that the statistics which followed are not accurate. How can you go from 59 members to zero in one year and close the doors?

When Phineas Bresee started the first Nazarene Church in Los Angeles the charter membership was reported as 135. When Crossroads was organized no charter members were mentioned. When Orchard Ridge was organized, no charter members were shown. I don't know if this is some kind of trend or what. I note that on the Indianapolis District in 2002, Harvest Point was organized with 67 charter members. First Hispanic was organized with 21 charter members.

Perhaps not mentioning charter members in the Eastern Michigan minutes is a trend started by W.W., who "pays no homage to the past!" The first mention of members appears in the 2003 minutes which is one year later than when Crossroads was organized.

In 2003, W.W. had left. The new pastor reported an average of 114 in morning worship and 6 members. In that year, the District finally bought a parsonage after about 23 years. Its estimated cost was $195,000.

In 2004, S.R. reported a membership of 47 members with an average morning worship attendance of 103. Then in 2005 and 2006 the membership and morning worship seemed to plateau at 55 members and 111 in attendance.

In 2007, a sharp downward spiral began in morning worship. Attendance dropped about 50%. Membership stagnated at 55 to 59. The plateau of 2005 and 2006 should have been a warning to the leadership that something was going wrong.

In the summer of 2009 it was reported that the pastor was retiring and the doors were shut. So the church that took one year to "found" on the work of others, died in 7 years! This was not reported in the District Minutes.

In my conversation with the assistant D.S. on Nov. 15, 2009, he indicated that S.R. did not really retire. Where he went, I do not know. In studying the history of S.R. in the District Minutes I discovered the same pattern. In his former pastorate at Round Rock we have an interesting scenario.

S.R., pastor at Round Rock
2002. Reports 77 members
2003 S.R. leaves and M.K.J. comes

> 2004 The church is listed as <u>inactive</u>
> 2005 The church is <u>disorganized.</u>
> The church died one year after S.R.. left!
> Crossroads died as S.R. left!

Yet, in a letter I received from S.A. dated Jan. 26, 2000, I share this excerpt. "I am asking the district to put significant money into helping us get a quality pastor and also looking toward acquiring a parsonage." To S.A.'s credit he did have the district buy a parsonage. As to a quality pastor, you be the judge!

So has all our work of the years evaporated? Have the seeds been blown away? I have a very dear friend who gave his best years to the Church of the Nazarene. He pastored some very large churches. Today, most of the churches he pastored are in steep decline. It gives him great agony!

The only glimmer of hope I have is that the assistant D.S. indicated that they plan to restart Crossroads. I only hope this is true. The Indianapolis D.S. told us in a letter that we were "clipping coupons" for our hard work in the years past. If it is shut down we wonder what kind of coupons will we be clipping?

"There has always been a tendency in the church considered as an earthly institution toward backsliding. It was so of ancient Israel. God said of them, "My people are bent on backsliding from me." Hos. 11:7. "It is so with the church today." Hogue, W.T. <u>History of the Free Methodist Church, 1915 vol. 1, p. 11</u>

Chapter Thirteen

Topsy Turvy

In October of 2006, the editor of H.T. would write to me. An excerpt from his letter states "From where I sit, there are numerous battles shaping up that have serious implications for our Zion. I trust we will never concede the authority of Scripture, the omniscience of God, and the message of heart purity to the objectors of such doctrine."

So I guess I am one of those hidden, innumeral battles that are raging over the landscape. This chapter will share insights into some of the currents that are sweeping over our church. It will reflect the trends in two Nazarene Districts. Throughout this book the paradigm of a pyramid is used. It is the author's theory that the "sending base" of a church needs to be stronger than the areas that receive the "benefits." In the case of Nazarenes, they are a missionary church which means they send missionaries, resources and money to world areas. At its inception, the Church of the Nazarene was always a church that believed in missions.

In 1980 the church passed legislation which changed its character forever. It became international in scope. This process has been ongoing for about 30 years. Progress has been slow, but momentum is beginning to catch up, perhaps in ways that had not been envisioned. At its last General Assembly the Assembly elected one if its General Superintendents from overseas.

Also overseas momentum began to supersede the momentum in the continental United States. This could end up with overseas sending missionaries to the U.S!

In the first chapter of this book I sketched a brief dateline of history starting with the Mayflower and leading up to the emergence of the Church of the Nazarene in the United States. This time line briefly traces the emergence of the Methodist Church. The Methodist Church began to gain momentum around 1730. By 1830 they were starting to change. Some historians feel that this is a reality after about 100 years of existence as a denomination. Around 1843 the Methodists began to have splits. The Wesleyan Methodist Church was formed. Shortly after this the Free Methodist Church emerged. By 1861 the Civil War began. Ten years later, Dwight L. Moody came on the scene. By 1880 the Holiness movement was beginning to take shape. In 1895 the Church of the Nazarene was organized. It thrived although it was still considered a minority group!

However, it is my prediction that history is about to repeat itself! I believe we are headed for a free fall! I will first share insights about the Indianapolis Nazarene District. For precise details the reader is referred to the Appendix pages 160-178.

It has always been the contention of the Church of the Nazarene that it needed to reproduce itself as strongly as possible. One arm for trying to do this was Home Missions, later called New Starts.

In the 1970's this was not a very strong effort. At least on the Eastern Michigan District with which I am familiar, it seemed to gain momentum in the first decade of the 21st century, perhaps because at least some Nazarenes perceived that they were failing in their mission.

I do not know when this trend started, but the Indianapolis District from 2000 used most of their funds under the Home Mission umbrella to prop up weak or dying churches. If it didn't happen as Home Mission it was called Emergency Assistance. Most of the expenditures were for churches that had been organized a long time but were sick or it trouble.

In the year 2000 this expenditure was about $79,237. It peaked out in 2003 with expenditures of $136,099. This included about $66,000 for New Starts. In 2006 there was a drastic, significant change. Home Mission and New Start was renamed Church Development. However, disbursements still continued to be made to churches that had existed for many years. One Hispanic church, at the time, got most of the disbursement.

It seems like a kind of shell game developed which interchanged the terms, inactive, merger, name change, new start, organized and disorganized. It became very difficult to track individual churches through this system.

Over the nine year period studied there was a loss of 12 organized churches. There was very little activity to start new churches. See appendix, active church list P. 170. The ratios of membership to attendance in the three major areas which are counted became inverted.

Variations in Nazarene statistics made this study extremely difficult. See page 173 of the appendix. Analysis of the finance of both districts shows an inverted pyramid according to the author's theory. p.175

The amount of resource put into Home Mission and New Start was very weak compared to where the rest of the effort and resource was put. The Eastern Michigan District engaged in much more effort in New Start than the Indianapolis District. See page 195 of the appendix.

The cost to lose members was monumental in the case of the Indianapolis District. See page 176 of the appendix. No matter how you study the effort of this army of Nazarenes over nine years it spells FAILURE in mission. The reports of the D.S. will corroborate what the author found out.

In 2000, "our lack of growth and enthusiasm for Sunday School continues to be of grave concern to me." Lee "It is time we quit bathing ourselves with church growth philosophy and quit worshipping at the thrones of George Barna, Rick Warren, Bill Hybels, Leith Anderson and many more." Lee

In 2001 under goals: "We have a host of smaller churches that are getting smaller. They have little or no leadership concerning Sunday School and musicians, and few or no youth are attending." Lee

"My goal, under the guidance of the Advisory Board and an Assessment Committee, is to plant three new churches in the next four years." Lee

2002, "This year we planted two new churches. I am hopeful to organize two more new churches this assembly year giving us four in two years." Lee

2003, "The devil is having hey-day with what is going on in many of our churches around the world today." " The church that I love is not perfect." Lee

2004, "I am concerned about the negative numbers in Sunday School and our responsibility lists." "The one statistic that deeply troubles me is a decrease in new Nazarenes." Lee

2005, "Pastors and laymen, it is imperative that we start new churches on the Indianapolis District." "I held town hall meetings in churches that were not pleasant for anyone in attendance. I had laymen in some of our churches who were hurt and pastors and parsonage families who had been verbally wounded and were hurting badly." "I dealt with staff problems this year and broken relationships, which are never pleasant. Several pastors resigned from their churches with no place to go." Lee

2006, "It is discouraging to realize that eleven of our churches did not take one person into church membership by profession of faith. For the first time in eleven years, we showed a decline of 31 in church membership, Ten of our churches remain the same as last year, and 35 churches showed a decline in membership." "The statistics concerning morning worship attendance are heartrending." "Every church, with God's help, must take in at least one person this year by profession of faith,. After all, this is our purpose for existence." Lee

2007, "Average morning worship attendance was 7,390. a decrease pf 255. I applaud every church that received new Nazarenes, but my heart is heavy when I realize that 15 of our congregations did not receive one new person into the fellowship of their church." Lee

2008, "It hurts me to say this, but for the past three years we have shown little or no growth. This is on a district that four decades ago, was in the top five of Sunday School attendance in our entire denomination. Yet, in spite of what I consider positive and civil changes <u>something is not right</u>: We are not growing and we do not have a compassion for the lost as in days gone by!" [53]

Even as this is written a movement is underway to have the Indianapolis District <u>reunite</u> with Southwest Indiana District. We are now touting the benefits of reuniting. We must put a positive spin on this. The fact is, this is a retrenchment and an indicator that in a Bible belt state the Church of the Nazarene is not meeting its goals. Why? There are many reasons. More on that later.

Let's look at the Eastern Michigan District. Its effort in Home Missions and New Starts is much more transparent than the Indianapolis District. You could say that the period 2003-2005 could be characterized by intense activity in church plants, mission churches and church status. The reader is invited to refer to the appendix pages 188, 193. The year 2003 seems to be the year of greatest activity for the period under study. Kudos are in order for this district. They did give it the old "college try!"

Eastern Michigan played the old shell game by bouncing around terms like, inactive, merger, name change, new start, disorganized and organized. This made it very difficult to track individual churches.

The observation can be made that Eastern Michigan was much more aggressive in New Starts and Home Missions than was the Indianapolis District. However, both districts disorganized about the same number of churches. The survival rate of New Starts in Eastern Michigan was very small, with survival in doubt for many who made it to 2009. Large sums of money were spent on New Starts. In 2009, Eastern Michigan had 15 less organized churches than it did in 1972. p. 189 in the appendix.

Let's look at attendance. Morning worship attendance in Eastern Michigan was over 100% of reported membership. What does this mean? Do they have a lot of attendees at morning worship who are not members? Do their counters grossly over count attendance? I don't know, but there is something wrong here!

Sunday evening used to be a mainstay service in the Church of the Nazarene. It fell like a meteor on this district! See appendix p. 190, 191. Sunday School was also in decline. Both of these services show an inverted pyramid. Except for morning worship all pyramids are inverted.

On both districts under study, the year 2006 seemed to be a pivotal year when most efforts at New Starts and Home Missions seemed to decline rapidly. See appendix p. 195. PP. 175, 176 of the appendix will give the reader another graphic look at both districts.

Eastern Michigan had an anomaly that the Indianapolis District did not have. This was churches with pastors under appointment by the D.S. See appendix pps. 196, 197 for details on this. These 25 churches represent a large block of weakness in the 65 active churches reported by Eastern Michigan. [54]

In summary, two districts in the Church of the Nazarene are not as strong as they appear to be. The Indianapolis District is losing in all areas and thus the thrust to reunite with Southwestern Indiana.

Both districts continue to wring out of their constituents, a high level of financial support in terms of their memberships. The author believes this is creating stress and unhealthy attitudes.

Both districts disorganized about the same number of churches over the period studied. Both districts have many very weak churches. The membership gravitates to the large churches.

A mainstay service, the Sunday evening service, is dying rapidly in both districts. Sunday School attendance is also in decline.

Both districts are using athletics in larger churches to build or maintain attendance. In some cases, soccer award Sunday has replaced morning worship. There are also basketball Sundays. Super bowl Sunday is another one. As Nazarenes, are we losing our way?

The author maintains that the base of the pyramid must be stronger than the top. This means new and growing churches to support the insatiable appetite of the International Church.

Now let us look at the International Church. Here are some international statistics reported in the denominational periodical by the general secretary. In the July-Aug. issue 2009 we reported 1,837,393 members for the end of the church year 2008 – 2009. In the Nov.–

Dec. issue of 2009 (three months later) we reported 1,829,373 members. This would be a discrepancy of 8,020 members.

In the same paragraph we reported a gain of 575,961 new Nazarenes for the quadrennium 2005-2008. We also reported 1,496,296 members for 2005. If you add the new Nazarenes to the 1,496,296 members reported for 2005 you get 2,072,257 members. Yet we claimed 1,837,296 members. If the 575,961 members is correct, then the 1,496,296 members reported for 2005 is wrong. This would make membership in 2005 1,261,432 instead of the 1,496,296 members reported. So no matter how you figure there are 234,864 members not accounted for in this paragraph.[55]

We reported on page 8 of H.T. for the July-Aug. issue of 2009, statistics which reflect 1,837,393 members at the end of 2008-2009 reporting year. On the same page we reported 1,496,292 members for 2005. Do the subtraction. This is a gain in members of 341,097. Yet in the same paragraph we claimed 575,961 new Nazarenes. This is a discrepancy of 234,864 members! We never seem to talk about or report our net membership. Again, this seems to reflect a significant "bleeding" in our membership.[56]

Page 39 of the July-Aug. issue 2009 has 2 paragraphs that start with 1994. One advances forward for the next 14 years. It has its set of statistics which bring us to 2008-2009. The claim here is for 429,000 members in WMAs.

The next paragraph also starts with 1994 to the end of this quadrennium which would be 2008-2009. The claim in this paragraph is that we have 1,178,991 members in World Mission Areas. Which figure is right? I don't know! This is a disparity of 749,991 members. On the same page we claim that in 2007 and 2008 we took in over 100,000 members a year in World Mission Areas.[57]

Also, in our statistical wanderings we seem to have trouble delineating between membership in WMAs and total world membership. We also have trouble clarifying the difference between a CTM and a truly organized church.

On page 30 of the Nov. – Dec. 2008 issue we have fast facts. The first column is about world areas. The second column lists statistics on organized churches. I don't know if this includes the whole world or just the six mission regions.[58] At any rate it seems to be in conflict with statistics given on page 39 in the July - Aug. issue of 2009. The third column shows membership. Again it is not clear. Does this mean total WMA membership or worldwide membership? If it is worldwide membership for the end of the 2008-2009 year, then it is in conflict with other statistics. Namely, those reported as follows:

1. 1,733,772 members in the 2008 Nov. – Dec. issue, P. 30.[59]
2. 1,837,393 members in the 2009 July – Aug. issue, P. 8.[60]
3. 1,829,373 members in the 2009 Nov.-Dec. Issue, P. 30.[61]

In terms of international membership we have an inverted pyramid based on the author's theory that the sending base should be larger than the receiving areas.

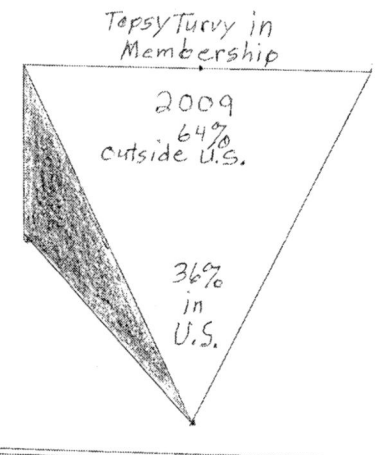

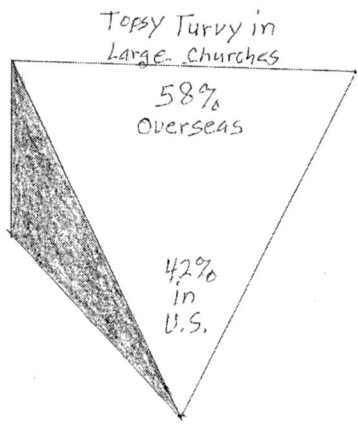

Top
Topsy Turvy in Membership

Bottom
58% overseas 42% in U.S.

In the Sept. – Oct. 2009 issue of H.T., membership gains in large churches in the Church of the Nazarene were reported. These gains were from 1985 – 2008. Again, we see a Topsy Turvy view.

58% overseas 42% in U.S.

Thus, sending churches reflect a smaller number of large churches. Namely, the U.S. where the church originated has smaller numbers of large churches. A larger percentage of large churches in the receiving areas of the church indicates the base is being inverted. In the author's view this is unhealthy. If this trend continues we might as well move the world headquarters overseas, and make the U.S. a mission field![62]

Let's look at schools. Schools are listed in six categories: They are: Graduate Seminaries and Theological Colleges, Liberal Arts Universities and Colleges with graduate programs, Undergraduate Liberal Arts Colleges, Undergraduate Seminaries and Theological Colleges, Certificate and Diploma Bible Colleges, and Specialized Training Schools. Of course, the service of these schools to membership will not be equal. Again, this is Topsy Turvy.

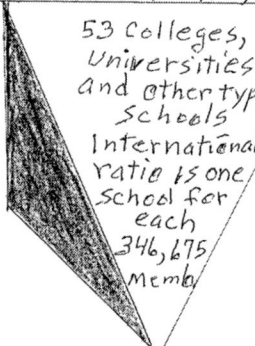

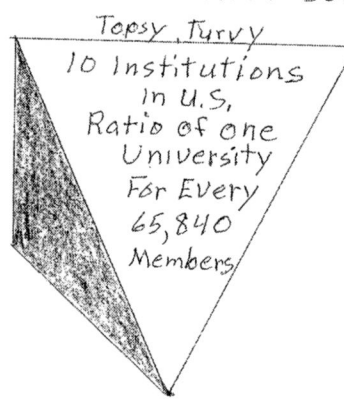

Top
International Ratio for Schools

Bottom
U.S. National Ratio for Schools

Churches are expected to support the schools. If the sending base is narrower than the receiving area it will put undue stress on the sending base. This is what creates a Topsy Turvy situation. Under Nazarene structure, it puts more financial stress on that base!

Let's look at education in the U.S. for a moment. Nazarenes have seven universities and one college in the U.S. They have one Bible College and one Graduate Seminary making a total of 10 institutions. This means that in theory each institution services 65,840 members. Or we can say that about 661,461 members are serviced by ten institutions. In the author's view this is way top heavy and creates an unrealistic pressure on local churches.[63]

10 Universities in U.S.

Financially, the churches are pressured to support their regional college plus the Seminary and the Bible College.

Let's take an in depth look at our school situation. First Nazarene institutions are highly successful. This attracts many students from outside Nazarene ranks, as the church fails in its mission to win men and women to Christ the Nazarene student body shrinks. See what is happening in the appendix pg. 205, 206.

As our Nazarene student body shrinks, universities are forced to recruit from other sources to continue to be successful. Once the Nazarene student body at a given campus shrinks to below 50% we are on a downward spiral in terms of Nazarene values. Historically, what happens to institutions is well documented.

The next concern has to do with the money churches are forced to pay in their budgets to the colleges. Does all this money end up benefiting Nazarene students? I doubt it! If a college takes federal money it cannot practice discrimination. Therefore, if a college is in that situation it forces Nazarene churches to help subsidize the education of non-Nazarene students. This may force us to ask some hard questions and make some painful decisions in the future.

In H.T., P.37 July-Aug., 2009, when Nazarenes discuss attendance they claim that 70% of worshippers are in 30% of their churches, and that 70% of their churches contain 30% of their members. Graphing this would make it look this way.[64]

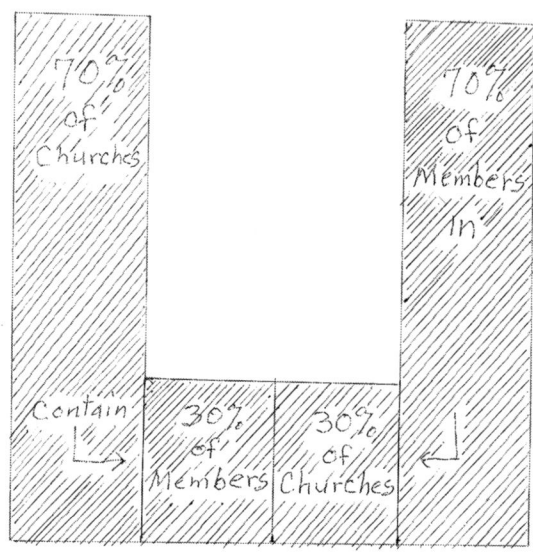
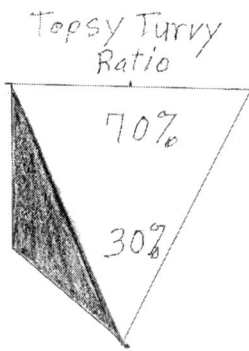

70/30 Ratio

Nazarenes also say that 30% of their pastors are bi-vocational. Logically, one would think that these pastors would serve in the 70% of the churches that contain 30% of the members. If only 30% are bi-vocational then how do the remaining 40% of pastors in small churches support themselves? Perhaps their wives support them![64] Having been bi-vocational I would say that the denomination kind of looks down on you although they need you.

A few years ago W.D, in Pensions and Benevolence, took away a large chunk of benefit for widows of bi-vocational pastors. In fact, when and if my wife becomes a widow, she will get 50% of what we were promised when we actively worked for the church. This was given to full-time pastors. This seems to smack of something! If the Nazarenes didn't have bi-vocational pastors where would they be?

So the Church of the Nazarene is faced with many dilemmas today! Its U.S. membership seems to be shrinking. Its overseas membership is increasing. Its Sunday School attendance is in decline at least in the two districts studied. In many cases Sunday Evening services are non-existent. Athletics and sports are touted as a tool of evangelism. The undergraduate student bodies of its colleges and universities reflect shrinking numbers of Nazarene students. In many cases, its historic doctrinal position is given lip service without a real experiential lifestyle.

In order to maintain an image of success it has often resorted to devious statistical methods. These include counting Easter Sunday morning worship as a part of Sunday School attendance, having athletic awards Sundays to beef up attendance, and other doubtful methods.

Another dilemma has to do with doctrine. Mark Quanstrom wrote a book called, **A Century of Holiness Theology.** In his introduction he states that the doctrine of John Wesley was reexamined. There were differences on key points and so the doctrine was reformulated. "This reformulation has resulted in two contemporaneous and competing definitions of entire sanctification in the Church of the Nazarene." This book was published in 2000 by Beacon Hill Press of Kansas City.

Quanstrom also stated that for half a century, from 1928 to 1976, the Church of the Nazarene's article on sanctification remained unchanged (p.137). In 1976 the church modified the article. In 1985 the word eradicate was removed from the Articles of Faith with respect to the church's doctrine of sanctification"[65]

It was in the 1985 General Assembly that a debate took place over the Article of Faith on sin. This debate promised to be a dilemma for the church. Wynkoop's book, A Theology of Love, brought this debate into full fruition. A Theology of Love, called into question the long–standing view of the church on sanctification.

The debate was perpetuated in the Seminary by men like Staples, Dunning and others. The result was that two streams of thought on one of the church's cardinal doctrines began to emerge from the Seminary. This started happening about 1982. Thus, the church had pastors going into the field with divergent views of sanctification. The damage this has done is incalculable![66] Article Ten underwent another revision at the last General Assembly in 2009. So Nazarenes are in trouble with their traditional doctrine.

Symptomatically of the many problems, the Indianapolis District had 40 unassigned, ordained elders on its roster in 2009. It had 7 ordained deacons unassigned. It had nine licensed ministers who were unassigned. This makes a total of 56 people on one district who are credentialed but unassigned. A few of these retired unassigned.

We don't seem to treat people in accord with our doctrine anymore. Perusal of district minutes indicates that people who had significant roles in the church are no longer Nazarenes. A very significant "bleeding" is ongoing in our church!

The condition of the church now suggests that several things could take place. (A) The base will continue to remain dormant. (B) The base will grow weaker and weaker until finally it will collapse. This could take years. (C) Finally, the base will not be able to support the top.

Obviously, we are not investing enough at the base in finance, training, prayer, blood, sweat and toil! Or perhaps we don't know how to win people to the Lord!

A revolutionary idea is that perhaps it is time to completely rethink how we present Jesus. Do we need 22,000 sq ft. recreational complexes (one church in Eastern Michigan) gymnasiums, fancy buildings, soccer programs, basketball leagues, Super Bowl

Sundays, huge maintenance programs, large campgrounds and other "hoopla" which accompanies running "church" today?

Is it time to hit the street, one-on-one, house-to-house, workplace-to-workplace, simple store fronts and whatever else it takes in utter simplicity to win men and women to Christ?

"Will you not give us life again, so that your people may rejoice in you? Show us your mercy, O Lord, and grant us Your salvation." PS. 85:6,7

Chapter Fourteen

What's Ahead?

Here is a page from a newspaper. (Mine) (The newspaper is fake – the content real. It ought to drive the Church of the Nazarene to its knees.) What will the future do? I am not sure, but as long as I draw breath, I will search for the truth. Like the Psalmist, I have chosen the way of truth. (Psalm 119:30).

21st Century News
Church of the Nazarene Implodes
Experts have many theories as to why

Double Standards

Before the information age the church could get away with different strokes for different folks. The standards were always different for 1st churches than for others. Club 25 churches could always do their own thing. It didn't matter if it was inside the frame work of the denomination or not! With the advent of the information age, everyone knows what everyone else is doing. This was a factor in the implosion of the church.

Jeremiah Prophet
Researcher

Immorality

At certain outstanding Nazarene universities ministerial students cut notches in their belts to show how many virgin's they have taken. Others light up their pipes and cigars as soon as they drive away from campus. Still others drink alcohol repeatedly on the way through their studies; others learn the fine art of lying. Others get involved in hazing rituals which are inappropriate for Christians.

Isaiah Watchman
Researcher

Politics

District Superintendents were putting relatives and friends into strategic positions in the church and calling it God's will. Other officials placed relatives and friends in positions which would lead to the "top." These were contributing factors.

Daniel Groans
Researcher

A Divided Seminary

Nazarenes can't make up their minds about their doctrine so they vacilate. There are divergent streams of thought coming out ot the Seminary with respect to the denomination's position on Holiness. Therefore its ministers present divergent views to their congregations.

Jacob Worm
Researcher

Evangelist Hash

Although there is a large pool of Nazarene Evangelists, many pastors practice the art of inviting district superintendents or even Generals to hold their revivals. This practice is called "Greasing the skids" to get to the "top." It also leaves able bodied evangelists sitting on the sidelines.

Amos Sad
Researcher

The Budget Dilemma

The only way to survive is to pay the budget. It is common knowledge that pastoring your way to success is to be sure your budgets are paid. You are a nothing unless dues are paid in full.

Thomas Shortchange
Researcher

Immorality Among Ministers

Yes, they fell like cold winter snow. They cohabited with their secretaries their organists, and others. When they were found out it cast a spell over the church. Often the solution was to transfer them to another district or state. Still others were not found out by man But it worked like a cancer inside the church. Factors like this fed the implosion.

John Revelator
Researcher

Falling From Inside

Yes, the decay started on the inside. It was so gradual that it was hardly noticed by many. The voices of others who noticed were speedily silenced until the implosion finally took down the outer shell and the whole structure collapsed! Heaven Wept!

Eli Ichabod
Researcher

I have searched a lifetime for truth. I can say with David the Psalmist, "As the hart pants after the water brook, so my soul pants after you, O God." (Psalm 42:1)[67]

At the dawn of the Reformation in England people were searching for truth. The church was telling them one thing and those who could read "smuggled in" New Testaments from Holland were reading a different story from God's word. In the novel, <u>Peter the Apprentice</u>, I share an excerpt. "We know not what to believe in these evil days," he said; "The gospellers say they have found the truth which the church has sought to hide all these years, and the church says the gospellers are heretics to be chased from the earth by fire and sword."[68]

Yes, who do we believe when the church presents to us men and women who teach us to live one way, but then they live a different way. Ways that do not ring true to scripture.

Many, many people have lost their way in the face of experiences that this book reveals. I think of the experiences which Austin Miles talks about in his book, <u>Don't Call Me Brother</u>. As a result of these experiences in a church, he lost his way and went from being an ordained minister to becoming a nonbeliever. The stories in his book can be validated. He speaks of religion's flip side and the spiritual desert which exists in America's churches.

He sums his book by saying, at the moment, the Church of Jesus Christ sits on a rotting foundation. All other churches built on the existing foundations will crumble as well. The only way for the church truly to serve God is to level completely what presently exists, rebuild the foundation, and start all over. This will require a total house cleaning, and church reform. At present, there are too many difficulties, too many people involved with wrong motives to insure a successful conclusion.

It may be that the church will be silenced altogether for a few years, with a total "falling away." God may see that as necessary, while He waits for a new generation to emerge! Young people He can work through, a generation that will bring back honesty and integrity. As a new breed of ministers rises up, we may finally be able to hear what Christ really wanted to say, in a church without "spot or blemish."[69]

In the aftermath of Christ Community (Crossroads) I find a scattered flock. Many have lost their way spiritually. Others have left the Church of the Nazarene because of its Topsy Turvy condition and have gone elsewhere trying to keep their faith.

Yes, we have faced betrayal in the church. We have faced lies, outright metaphorical assassinations, betrayal, and disappointments. We have faced the ridicule of "shunning." After working our hearts out for God and the Church of the Nazarene we have been <u>exiled</u>!

The Church of the Nazarene is about one hundred years old and is trembling on the verge of losing its way. "Someone has said that a reform seldom outlives the lives of the reformers. We are glad to note that, while all of those who were most prominent in the beginning of this movement have passed away, other hearts and hands are actively engaged in maintaining the same standard of unworldly and aggressive Christianity."[70] The latter statement was made in 1915. What would the author say if he saw his church today?

It would seem to me that the church has to reinvent itself about once a century to maintain its vigor, growth and spirituality.

While our experiences at Clintonville and Christ Community in Michigan and at First Church in Indianapolis, Indiana have thrown serious doubts of faith into our pathways, we have come too far to turn back in our faith now. Sailors that we are, our anchor holds!

We know that there is a church within the church. We know that Christ said, "Beware of false prophets who come to you in sheep's clothing, for within they are ravening wolves." Matt 7:15."[71] Not every one who says to me, Lord, Lord, shall enter into the kingdom of heaven; but the one who is doing the will of My Father, Who is in heaven." Matt7:21.[72]

A year after my Dad passed away I wrote him a letter. I know it sounds odd, but I have a feeling from somewhere out there he read it!

Oct. 12, 1988

Dear Dad:

Well Dad, it's just been a year since you left us and went to be with the Lord. Dad, when I stand beside your grave I get this warm feeling through my whole body . . . like you are not that far away!

Dad, I remember so many things you taught us. . . your consistent and steady faith in God – a God of love and justice . . . the hymns you used to sing behind the wheel of the car as we were traveling down the road . . .the good that you saw in each of we children . . . the times when you tried to purge the naughtiness out of us, but with love . . . our family prayer time . . . waiting for you to come home from selling Christmas Trees in Detroit at Christmas time . . . the hunts we took together . . . the tough conditions you labored under so many times . . . the influence of your life hangs over us like a shadow . . . A shadow of things to come . . . your prayers follow us like the hound of heaven . . .

Dad, sometimes I think that I am not doing so well down here . . . but I really try . . . I worry about some of us whom you loved dearly and prayed so hard for all your life . . . sometimes, I worry that I might not have done my best for God . . . but when those thoughts come I ask my heavenly Father to see me through the storms as He did you . . . I think of the renewed covenant I made with you two weeks before you left us . . . and Dad I want you to know again, that I am following your footsteps **HOME!**.

Love,
Your son, Wayne Gordon

To all whose hopes have been dashed by events, people and places inside the earthly church God invites you back. These words say it well.

"Stand then in His great might,
With all His strength endued;
But take to arm you for the fight,
The panoply of God;

> *That having all things done*
> *And all your conflicts passed,*
> *Ye may o'er come thro Christ alone*
> *And <u>stand</u> entire at last."*[73]

There is an ancient poem written by Edward Sill. It is titled "Opportunity." It tells of a furious battle in the days of swords. A prince's banner wavers and is knocked backwards. It seems to be hemmed in by its foes.

A cowardly soldier hangs on the battle's edge. He thinks, "My sword is dull and worthless. If I had a sword like the King's son I could turn this battle around! But my sword is blunt and worthless." He snaps the blade in two and throws it down. He then sneaks away from the battle.

But the prince comes along. He is wounded and has no weapon. He sees the broken sword, he picks it up and with a heroic shout he hews the enemy down and saves a great cause that day.

Sometimes, we don't have much in a battle. In a spiritual battle we may only have opportunity and the grace that God gives us to stand when we are wounded. And so we maintain our faith.

And so we <u>STAND!</u>

Appendix Index

Indianapolis District pp. 160 - 178

Tracking Individual Churches	160 – 167
Summary of Church Status	169
Net Active Church List	170
Attendance Patterns	171
Pyramid View – Churches, Members, Attendance and Finance	172
Variables Examples	173
Home Missions Finance	174
Two District Finance Comparison	175
Financial Comparison	176
Statistical Comparison on Membership – Two Districts	177 – 178

Eastern Michigan District pp. 179 – 204

Tracking Individual Churches	179 – 187
Summary of Church Status	188
Net Active Church List	189
Attendance Patterns	190
Pyramid View – Churches, Members, Attendance and Finance	191
Variables Examples	192
Church Plants or Mission Churches	193
Churches in Transit (graphs)	194
Financial Support – Home Missions, New Starts	195
Requirements for Pastoral Appointments	196 – 198
Eastern Michigan History	199
Examples of D.S. Exaggerations on Two Districts	200 – 202
Attendance and Finance	203 – 204

International Church pp. 205 - 206

Rank in Number of Nazarene Students on Campus	205 - 206

Appendix
Indianapolis District
Nazarene
Tracking Individual Churches
2000

	Home Mission Payout
Carthage – org. 1950	6,350
Indianapolis Door of Hope – org. 1990	28,870
Indianapolis Jester Memorial – org. 1983	2,006
Richmond New Life – org. 1982	6,600
Richmond Southview – org. 1941	13,016
Indianapolis Fall Creek – org. 1922	3,336
Emergency Assistance	11,839
Rushville – org. 1945	2,020
Vevay – org. 1952	5,200
Under <u>Allocated</u> Funds listed 72 churches	$79,237

Summary

Listed 72 churches in Church Directory — 1 New Start

Net = 72 organized churches — Eastside – org. 1945

Unknown what was started – Whole Person Ministries?

2001

Greens Fork – org. 1935 – <u>Inactive</u>
Greenfield Grace – org. 1959 – <u>Merged</u> – to Greenfield First
Indianapolis Grace Pointe – <u>Name Change</u>
Indianapolis Meridian Street – org. 1945 –<u>Merged</u> with
Indianapolis Trinity – org. 1993 –<u>Merged</u> Cornerstone
Westbrook – <u>Merged</u> – Grace Pointe

	Home Mission Payout
Carthage – org. 1950	$ 6,050
Door of Hope – org. 1990	31,612
Fall Creek – org. 1922	3,913
Jester Memorial – org. 1983	2,467
Richmond New Life – org. 1982	4,785

Richmond Southview – org. 1941	12,780
Rushville – org. 1945	1,645
Vevay – org. 1952	3,265
Emergency Assistance	<u>32,420</u>
	$98,937

<u>Assisted These Churches</u>
Brooklyn, Connersville, Door of Hope, Indianapolis Trinity, Shepherd Community, Indianapolis Northside, Osgood, Triton Central, United Community, Vevay, Rushville.
Under <u>Allocated</u> Funds listed 70 churches

Listed 70 churches in Church Directory	<u>Summary</u>
Net – 66 churches	1 Inactive
	4 Mergers
	1 Name Change

Appendix
Indy – Con't.
Nazarene
2002

Greens Fork – org. 1935 – <u>Disorganized</u>
Greenwood – org. 1967 – <u>Disorganized</u>
Door of Hope - org. 1990 – <u>Disorganized</u>
Greenwood – org. 1967 – <u>Name Change</u>
Meadowbrook – 1947 <u>Merged</u> – Indianapolis Southwest
*First Hispanic – org. 2002 – <u>Organized</u> – (Ritter)
*Harvest Point – org. 2002 – <u>Organized</u>

	Home Mission **<u>Payout</u>**
Carthage – org. 1950	$ 5,600
Door of Hope – org. 1990	29,435
Fall Creek – org. 1922	4,905
Richmond New Life – org. 1982	4,620
Richmond Southview – org. 1941	13,756
Rushville – org. 1945	660

Vevay – org. 1952	1,321
<u>Emergency Assistance</u>	
Cambridge City – org. 1921	1,400
Greens Fork – org. 1935	2,519
Jester Memorial – org. 1983	2,161
Ludlow Hill – org. 1973	1,607
Shepherd Community – org. 1963	1,925
United Community – org. 1965	2,000
Cornerstone – org. 2001	<u>46,835</u>
Under <u>Allocated</u> Funds listed 68 churches	$118,744

Listed 68 churches in the Church Directory
Net = 64 churches

<u>Summary</u>
2 Organized
1 Merger
1 Name Change
3 Disorganized

Appendix
Indy – Con't.
Nazarene
2003

	Home Missions **Payout**
Carthage – org. 1950	$ 4,488
Door of Hope – org. 1990	22,686
Fall Creek – org. 1922	6,379
Richmond New Life – org. 1982	2,185
Richmond Southview – org.1941	7,398
First Hispanic – org. 2002 (Ritter)	<u>19,593</u>
	62,729

Carthage – org. 1950 – <u>Disorganized</u>
Indianapolis Ritter – org. 1943 – <u>Disorganized</u>
Mount Zion – org. 1966 – <u>Inactive</u>
Harvest Point at Greenwood – org. 2002
North Myrtle Beach, The Bridge – <u>New Start</u> – <u>CTM</u> – 2003

New Hope – <u>org. 2003</u> – <u>New Start</u>

<u>Emergency Assistance</u>
Greens Fork – org. 1935	$ 460
Jester – org. 1983	2,931
Greens Fork – org. 1935	361
Vevay – org. 1952	10
Fall Creek – org. 1922	5,647
Shepherd Community - org. 1963	1,500
New Hope – org. 2003	2,000
Indy Ritter – org. 1945	14,638
New Start	1,064
New Starts/Churches	<u>44,759</u>
Under <u>Allocated</u> Funds listed 66 churches	$136,099

Listed 66 churches in Church Directory
Listed 70 churches under membership
Net = 63

<u>Summary</u>
2 Disorganized
1 Inactive
2 New Start
1 Organized

Appendix
Indy Con't.
Nazarene
2004

	Home Missions **<u>Payou</u>**t
Hispanic – Ritter – org. 1945 (New)	$21,475
Hispanic – Shepherd – org. (New) 2004	15,037
Richmond New Life – org. 1982	2,057
Richmond Southview – org. 1941	<u>6,667</u>
<u>Emergency Assistance – P.88</u>	$45,236
Carthage – org. 1950	$27

Topsy Turvy in The Church of the Nazarene

Centerville – org. 1950	200
Door of Hope – org. 1990	368
Fall Creek – org. 1922	7,182
Franklin – org. 1941	1,000
Jester Memorial – org. 1983	771
Victorious Life – org. 2004	5,378
Meadowbrook – org. 1947	2,704
New Hope – org. 2003	1,830
Osgood – org. 1955	2,316
Rushville – org. 1945	5,646
Shepherd Community – org. 1963	11,466
Speedway – org. 1944	6,420
New Starts	<u>13,256</u>
	$58,564
Total	$103,800

Victorious Life – <u>Organized</u> – org. 2004
Lawrence – <u>Name Change</u>
Lawrence & Fall Creek – <u>Dead</u> – Both merged into Victorious Life
Under <u>Allocated</u> Funds listed 65 churches
Listed 67 churches in the Church Directory
Net – 65 churches
Differences reflect Nazarene reporting

<u>Summary</u>
1 Merger
2 Disorganized
1 Organized
2 New Starts

Appendix
Indy – Con't
Nazarene
2005

Home Missions
Payout

Indianapolis First Hispanic – org. 2002	$18,647
Richmond New Life – org. 1982	2,226
Richmond Southview – org. 1941	6,072
Whole Person Ministries – org. CTM	15,704
Victorious Life – org. 2004	12,336
Osgood – org. 1955	2,800

Emergency Assistance

Richmond First – org. 1916	7,000
Door of Hope – org. 1990	3,593
Jester Memorial – org. 1983	826
Richmond Southview – org. 1941	904
Andersonville Repairs? – org.	2,660
Shepherd Community – org. 1963	2,400
Northside – org. 1920	1,447
	$76,615

New Starts
Grace Harbor – CTM Mission - 2005
Grace Point Hispanic – CTM Mission - 2005
Promised Land – CTM Mission – 2005
Whole Person Ministry – CTM Mission – 2005
Under Allocated Fund listed 63 churches
Listed 67 churches in the Church Directory
Which includes 4 CTMs
 Net = 67 churches

Summary
4 New Start

Appendix
Indy – Con't.
Nazarene
2006

Avon Community to Avon Parkside – <u>Name Change</u>
Mooresville to Life Pointe Community – <u>Name Change</u>
Laurel - <u>Disorganized</u> – org. 1935
Promise Land – <u>Dropped</u> – started 2005
Grace Harbor – <u>CTM Mission</u> - started 2005
Indianapolis Grace Pointe Hispanic – <u>CTM Mission</u> – 2005
Indianapolis Whole Person Ministry – <u>CTM Mission – 2005</u>

	Budget
<u>First Hispanic</u> – org. -. 2002	
<u>Whole Person</u> - started - 2005	$20,000
<u>Emergency Assistance</u>	6,000
	20,000

No disbursements in minutes
Under <u>Allocated</u> Funds listed 64 churches
Listed 65 churches in Church Directory which included 3 CTMs

	<u>Summary</u>
Net = 63 churches including 3 CTMs	2 Name Changes
	1 CTM Dropped
	1 <u>Disorganized</u>

<u>2007</u>

Vevay to River Point - <u>Name Change</u>
Triton Central – <u>Disorganized</u>
Grace Harbor - <u>CTM Mission</u> – in allocated funds
Indianapolis Grace Pointe Hispanic Ministry – <u>CTM Mission</u> – started 2006
Indianapolis Whole Person Ministry - <u>CTM Mission</u> – 2005
<u>Under</u>
(New) <u>District Development Funds</u> – was Home Mission prior to 2006

First Hispanic – org. 2002	$18,000
Northside – org. 1920	30
Mount Zion – org. 1966	112

Vevay – org. 1952	252
Triton Central – org. 1967	500
Morristown – org. 1919	400
New Castle Southside – org. 1945	1,050
Whole Person – org. CTM 2005	2,200
Centerville – org. 1949	3,147
Madison – org. 1940	247
Avon – org. 1991	<u>1,800</u>
Under <u>Allocated</u> Funds listed 64 churches	$27,738

Listed 65 churches in Church Directory which included 3 CTMs
Net = 64 churches including 3 CTMs

<u>Summary</u>
1 Name Change
1 Disorganized

Appendix
Indy = Con't.
Nazarene
2008

New Hope – org. 2003 – <u>Disorganized</u>
*<u>District Development Funds</u> – was Home Mission
prior to 2006   <u>Church Development</u>

Hispanic Ministries – CTM Mission (Not Known)	$18,242
Whole Person – org. CTM 2007	1,200
Southport – org. 1943	300
Triton Central – org. 1967	4,082
College Corner – org. 1946	2,500
Speedway – org. 1944	1,825
Speedway – org. 1944	100
Stringtown – org. 1915	600
Vevay – org. 1952	754
Richmond New Life – org. 1982	550
New Hope – org. 2003	<u>1,210</u>
Under <u>Allocated</u> Funds listed 62 churches	$31,363

Listed 64 churches in Church Directory which
Included 3 CTMs

Net = 60 organized churches
Net loss of 12 churches over the period studied   <u>Summary</u>
                                                           1 Disorganized

Appendix
Indianapolis District
Nazarene
Summary Church Status
2000 – 2009

Inactive
1. Mount Zion
2. Greens Fork

2

Merger
1. Fall Creek to Lawrence, Lawrence and Fall Creek to Victorious Life – 2 died
2. Greenfield Grace to Greenfield First
3. Indy Meridian to Trinity to Cornerstone – 2 died
4. Indy Trinity to Cornerstone – 1 died
5. Meadowbrook to Indy Southwest
6. Westbrook to Grace Pointe

6

Name Change
1 Indianapolis Cornerstone
2. Westbrook
3. Lawrence
4. Avon Community
5. Mooresville
6. Vevay

6

New Start
1. New Hope
2. Harvest Point
3. The Bridge
4. First Hispanic
5. Promise Land

CTM
1. Grace Pointe Hispanic
2. Whole Person
3. Grace Harbor
4. Shepherd Hispanic

5 New Starts
3 are gone
2 are organized
1 is still a mission

Disorganized
1. Greens Fork
2. Greenwood
3. Door of Hope
4. Carthage
5. Ritter Avenue
6. Laurel
7. Promise Land
8. Triton Central
9. New Hope
10. Indy Northside
11. Mount Zion

11

New Starts
1. The Bridge – gone
2. Promise Land – gone

2

Total 13

Organized
1. First Hispanic
2. Harvest Point
3. Victorious Life
4. New Hope

4

Appendix
Indy – Con't
Nazarene
2000–2008
District Minutes
Indianapolis Nazarene
District
Net Active Church List
2000–2008 *

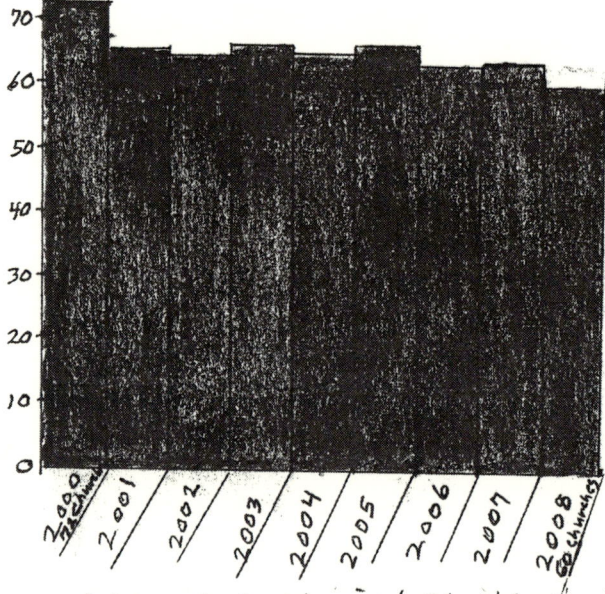

A loss of 12 organized churches
in the 9 years of this study.

Over this Period
Disorganized
1. Greens Fork
2. Greenwood
3. Door of Hope
4. Carthage
5. Ritter Ave.
6. Laurel
7. Promise Land
8. Triton Central
9. New Hope
10. Indy Northside
11. Mount Zion
12. The Bridge

Mergers
1. Westbrook
2. Greenfield Grace
3. Meadowbrook
4. Fall Creek
5. Indy Trinity
6. Lawrence

Summary
12 Dead

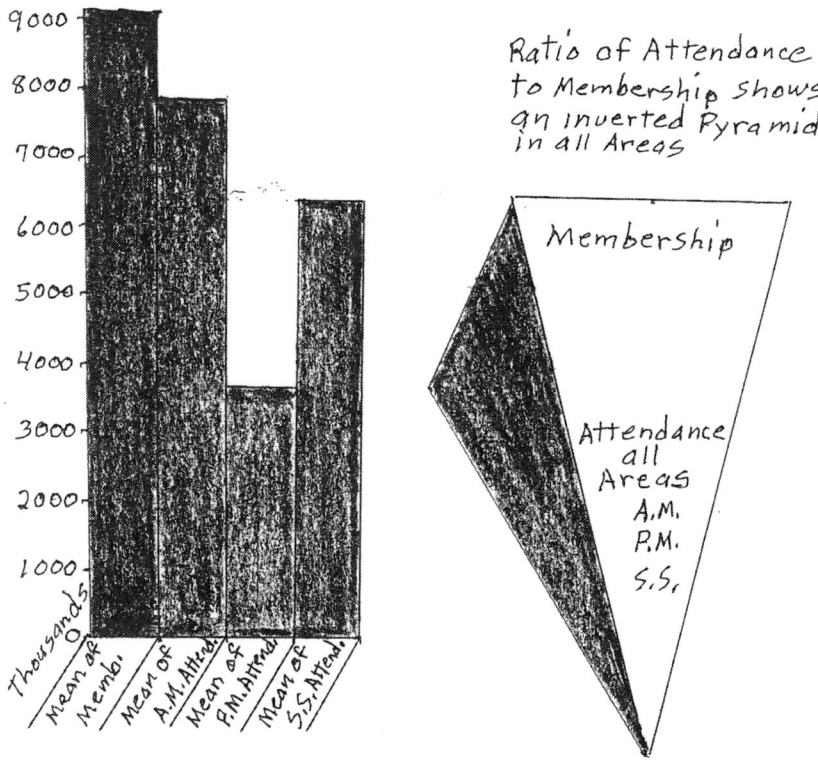

Topsy Turvy in The Church of the Nazarene

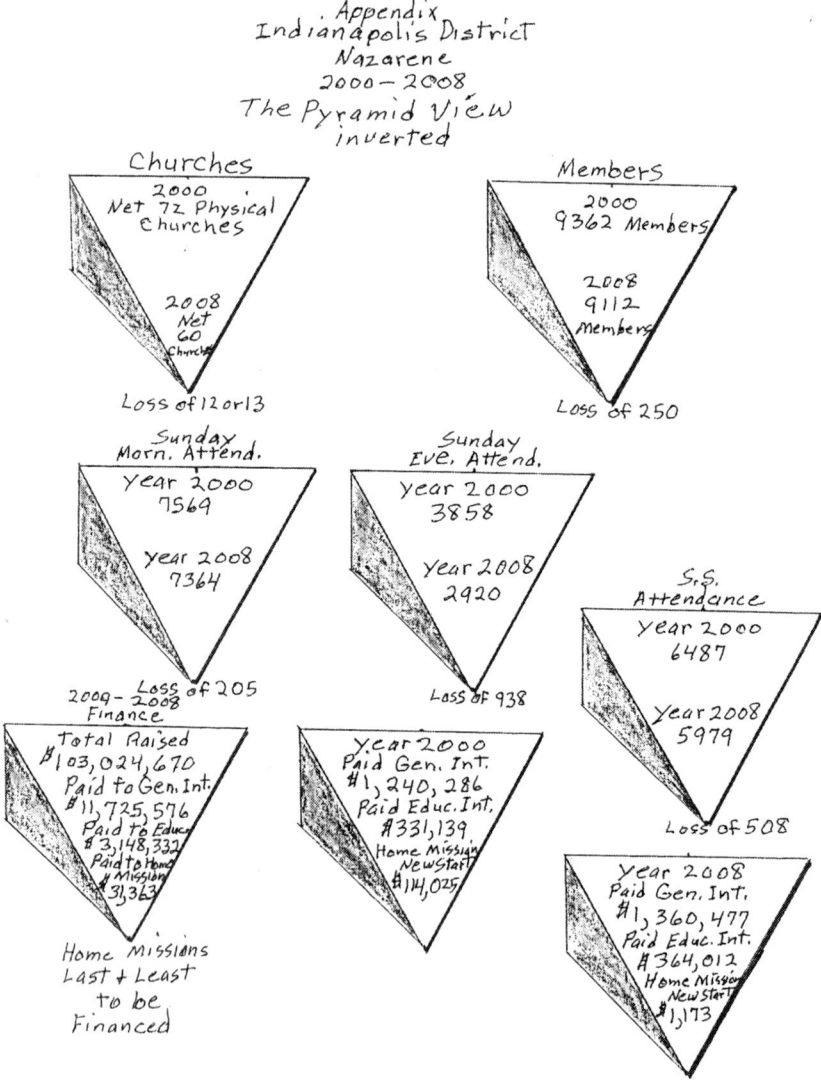

Examples of Variables
In Nazarene Reporting
Indianapolis District

Three Sources of Information
All Inside Nazarene Minutes

1. Home Mission Budgets and Disbursements
2. Financial and Statistical – Home Missions – VI
3. Paid District Interests – Home Missions and New Starts -2-A

Year	#1	#2	#3 Comb. Col. 11A & 11B
2000	$ 95,226	$147,920	$114,225
2001	105,256	147,060	119,474
2002	113,612	147,020	123,136
2003	88,277	139,428	123,740
2004	118,780	108,469	147,237
2005	108,160	106,345	127,967
2006	59,400	0	16,011
2007	58,900	*27,738	16,011 or 43,749
2008	0	*31,363	1,173

*District Development Funds – Direct aid to churches
None of these total Disbursement columns agree

Appendix
Indianapolis
District
Nazarene
2006-2008
Financial Support,
Home Missions and
New Starts

The collapse of support for Home Missions and New Starts beginning in 2006 cannot be blamed on poor economic conditions. During this time General Interest giving increased. So did giving to universities and colleges.

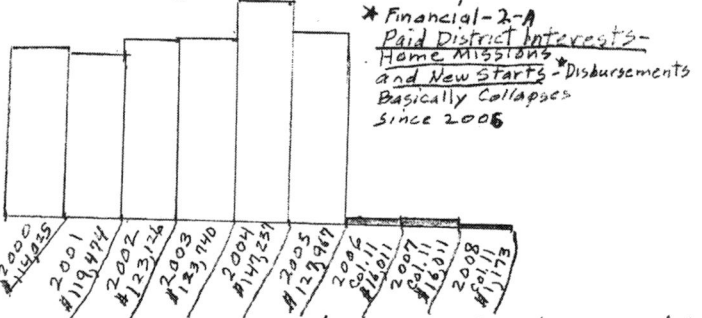

*Financial-2-A
Paid District Interests-
Home Missions
and New Starts *Disbursements
Basically Collapses
since 2006

2000 #14,435
2001 #19,494
2002 #23,126
2003 #23,040
2004 #47,251
2005 #23,949
2006 Col. 11 $0.11
2007 Col. 11 $0.11
2008 Col. 11 $1.73

*These figures reflect direct aid to New Starts and Home Missions. They do not reflect gifts to individuals and misc. items. These figures collected from Paid District Interests, Home Mission and New Start, Col. 11A and 11B Combined (Nazarene Minutes) Through 2005

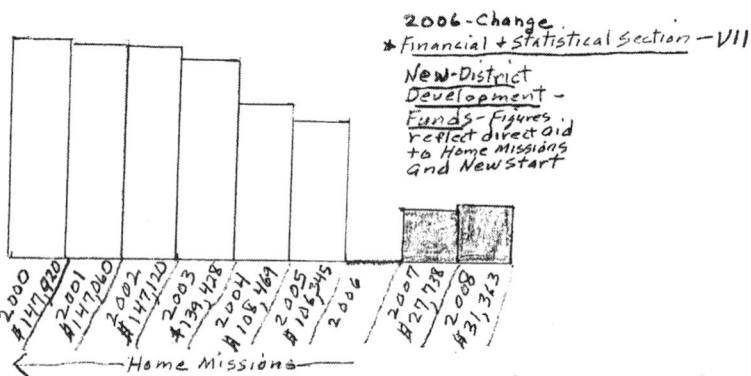

2006-Change
*Financial + Statistical Section —VII

New-District
Development-
Funds-Figures
reflect direct aid
to Home Missions
and New Start

2000 #141,040
2001 #147,040
2002 #147,120
2003 #139,428
2004 #108,469
2005 #106,345
2006
2007 #27,738
2008 #31,343

←——Home Missions——→

*These figures gleaned from same source (Nazarene Minutes) under Financial and Statistical Disbursements

Appendix
A Financial Comparison of TWO Nazarene Districts

Topsy Turvey Pyramids
2000-2008
Indianapolis District

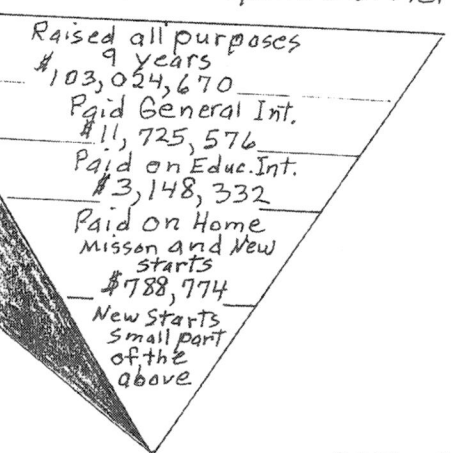

Raised all purposes 9 years
$103,024,670
Paid General Int.
$11,725,576
Paid on Educ. Int.
$3,148,332
Paid on Home Mission and New starts
$788,774
New Starts small part of the above

2002-2009
Eastern Michigan District

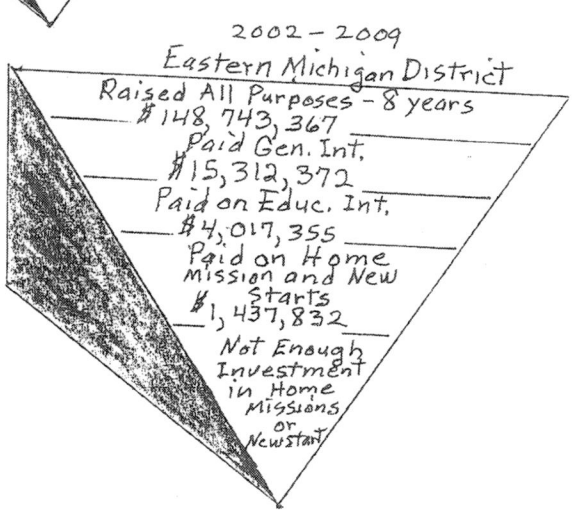

Raised All Purposes - 8 years
$148,743,367
Paid Gen. Int.
$15,312,372
Paid on Educ. Int.
$4,017,355
Paid on Home Mission and New starts
$1,437,832
Not Enough Investment in Home Missions or NewStart

Appendix
Financial Analysis
Consider Each District a Nazarene Army in the Field

1. Look at the Indianapolis District, taking out General interests it cost $91,299,094 for nine years of operation in the field. It cost this to lose a minimum of 250 members over the period of operation. Another way to look at it is that it cost $365,196 for each lost member over this nine year period. Does this reflect a victorious army?

2. Look at the Eastern Michigan District. They claimed to have gained 1311 members over 8 years. The cost of this was $133,458,975 taking out General interests. This means it cost them $101,799 for each new member gained during the 8 years studied. If we could say that a medium sized church might have about 164 members, then the cost to win 164 new people to Christ was $16,691,592. So it could cost $16,691,036 to create one medium sized church. In case you wonder how the latter figures were arrived at, here it is. The performance of this army was based on an average of 74 active churches over the 8 year period from 2002 – 2009. This district claimed a gain in membership of 1311. Just so the reader understands the math steps followed, here they are;

Step 1 – 74 active churches into 1311 members = 17.71 members. This means that each active church theoretically gained 17.716 members for 8 years.

Step 2 – 17.716 members divided by 8 years equals 2.214 members per year, per church.

Step 3 - 74 churches times 8 years equals 592 church years. 2.214 members per year *times* 592 church years equals 1310.68 members.

3. These statistics seem incredible even though one district showed modest growth.

4. From a business standpoint is this survivable or sustainable?

5. The Bible indicates that the major goal of the church on earth is to multiply. It also calls for the church to be good stewards.

6. So I guess we can go on spinning our wheels until we run out of gas!

Statistical Comparison on Membership Two Nazarene Districts

Indianapolis 2000-2009 | Eastern Michigan 2002-2009

Year	Memb	Inactive	Loss	Gain		Memb	Inactive	Loss	Gain	
2009	9070	1382	490	448		12725	1617	464	651	
2008	9112	1089	457	476		12538	1560	585	673	
2007	9060	1095	586	555		12450	1338	496	936	
2006	9060	1095	586	555		11990	676	575	771	
2005	9091	919	543	572		11994	743	428	541	
2004	9062	1096	543	580		11681	654	531	843	
2003	9025	864	737	676		11369	688	815	770	
2002	9355	931	670	624		11414	1009	660	855	
2001	9401	824	557	546						
2000	9362	1044	521	539						
	Total Loss -292	Total 10,339	Total 5,690	Total 5,621	Net Loss 69	Total Gain 1,311	Total 8,335	Total 4534	Total 6040	Net Gain 1506

Columns Do Not Agree — Columns Do Not Agree

Statistical Comparison on Membership Two Nazarene Districts

Statistical Comparison on Membership Two Nazarene Districts Con't.

Membership Minus Inactive Equals Net Membership

Year	Indianapolis 2000-2008 Total Memb.	Minus Inactive	Net Memb.	Year	Eastern Michigan 2002-2008 Total Memb.	Minus Inactive	Net Memb.
2009	9,070	1,382	7,688	2009	12,725	1,617	11,108
2008	9,112	1,089	8,023	2008	12,538	1,560	10,978
2007	9,060	1,095	7,965	2007	12,450	1,338	11,112
2006	9,060	1,095	7,965	2006	11,990	676	11,314
2005	9,091	919	8,172	2005	11,794	793	11,001
2004	9,062	1,096	7,966	2004	11,681	654	11,027
2003	9,025	864	8,161	2003	11,369	688	10,681
2002	9,355	931	8,424	2002	11,414	1,009	10,405
2001	9,401	824	8,577				
2000	9,362	1,044	8,318				
Totals	-292	27 Churches did not report Inactive members	-630 Mean Net Active Memb. 8,922		+1311		+703 Mean Net Active Memb. 10,953

Statistical Comparison on Membership Two Nazarene Districts Con't.

Appendix

Eastern Michigan
Nazarene
Tracking Individual Churches

2002

*Honey Creek – 47 members - Named in Apportionments - No directory name
Cornerstone – used to be Pine Grove – <u>Name Change</u>
*Crossroads – Used to be Christ Comm. – <u>Name Change</u> (Restart not New Start)
Crosswalk Comm. – used to be Westland – <u>Name Change</u>
Detroit New Hope
*Dundee – org. 2002
Everyword Ministries – org. 1958
Flint Abundant Grace
Flint Westgate – <u>inactive</u>
Harvest Comm.
Southwest
Sterling Heights – inactive – <u>Disorganized</u>
North Oaks – <u>inactive</u>
Becher Comm. – <u>Merged</u> to Flint First
Flint New Life – Formerly Flint Eastside – <u>Name Change</u>
<u>Apportionments</u> – 72 active, 2 inactive
Listed – 75 Churches
Net = 72 Churches

<u>Summary</u>
4 Name Changes
1 Inactive
1 Disorganized
1 Merger
2 Organized

Appendix

Eastern Michigan
Nazarene
2003

Anchor Bay – 131 members org. 1989
Ann Arbor Honey Creek – 49 members org. 1964
Chelsea – 19 members org. 1996
Cornerstone – 40 members – org. 1953, 1961
*Crossroads <u>Mission</u> 6 members org. 2002 – Christ Comm. <u>Restart</u>
Detroit New Hope – 47 members – org. 1982
Mount Morris – 49 members – org. 1953
Flint Westgate – <u>Disorganized</u>
North Oaks – <u>Disorganized</u>
Everyword Ministries – <u>Inactive</u>
*Armada Comm. – <u>Mission</u> – org. 2003
Clio Comm. – <u>Mission</u> – <u>New Start</u>
Flint New Life – <u>Mission</u> – <u>New Start</u>
Flushing Comm. – <u>Mission</u> – 55 members
Lake Comm. – <u>Mission</u> - <u>New Start</u>
Love Mercy Ministries – <u>Mission</u> – <u>New Start</u>
New Covenant – <u>Mission</u> – <u>New Start</u>
New Heights Comm. – <u>Mission</u> – Mt. Clemans – <u>New Start</u>
Northpointe – <u>Mission</u> – 22 members – <u>New Start</u>
Orchard Ridge – <u>Mission</u> – <u>New Start</u>

Apportionments Show 76 Active Churches
Listed – 76 churches
Net = 76 churches

<u>Summary</u>
2 Disorganized
10 Mission or New Start
1 Inactive
1 Organized 2003

Appendix
Eastern Michigan
Nazarene
2004

Anchor Bay – 131 members – org. 1989
Honey Creek – 53 members – org. 1964
*Armada – 37 members
Chelsea – 18 members – org. 1996
Cornerstone – 43 members – org. 1953, 1961
*Crossroads – 47 members – org. 2002 - (Restart)
Detroit New Hope – 54 members – org. 1982
Dundee – 14 members – org. 2002
Flint Abundant Grace – 46 members – org. 1990
Harvest Comm. – 21 members – org. 1943
Mount Morris – 45 members – org. 1953
Everyword Ministries – <u>Inactive</u> – org. 1958
Clio Comm. – no members listed – org. 2006
*Flat Rock – <u>inactive </u>– org. 1941
*Deer Park – <u>Mission</u> – New – old start (Restart)
Flint New Life - <u>Mission</u> – start 2003
Flushing Comm. – <u>Mission</u> – 78 members
Love Mercy – <u>Mission</u>
New Covenant – <u>Mission</u>
Orchard Ridge – <u>Mission</u>
Lake Comm. – <u>Disorganized</u>
New Heights Comm. – <u>Disorganized</u>
Northpointe – <u>Disorganized</u>

Apportionments Show 74 Active Churches plus 2 New Start (babies)
Listed - 69 churches
Net = 71 churches

<u>Summary</u>
3 Disorganized
2 Inactive
6 Missions

<u>Gone from List</u>
Northpointe
New Heights
Lake Comm.
Flat Rock – Inactive
Everyword Ministries – Inactive

*Note- (S.R.) pastor at Flat Rock - 2002 – shows 77 members, 2003 – shows 70 members (T.B.) 2004 – shows inactive . T.B. retired 2004 2005 - Disorganized Church died one year after S.R. left. Crossroads died the second time as S.R. left in 2009.

P. 55 D.S. Report claimed 4 new churches started. Orchard Ridge listed last year. New Covenant listed last year. Clio Comm. listed last year.
*Deer Park only 1 started –
This has been in and out since the 70s.

Appendix

Eastern Michigan
Nazarene
2005

Anchor Bay – 117 members – org. 1989
*Armada – 42 members
Chelsea – 20 members – org. 1996
Cornerstone – 42 members – org. 1953
Crossroads – 55 members
Detroit New Hope – 58 members – org. 1982
Dundee – 28 members – org. 2002
Flint Abundant Grace – 59 members
Harvest Comm. – 21 members – org. 1943
Living Water – 54 members – Ann Arbor – org. 1964
Mount Morris – 41 members – org. 1953
*Orchard Ridge – <u>No statistics</u> – org. 2005 – 122 A.M. attendance
Flat Rock – <u>Disorganized</u>
Everyword Ministries – <u>Inactive</u>
Clio Comm. – <u>No statistics</u>
Deer Park – <u>No statistics</u>
Flint New Life – <u>No statistics</u>
Flushing Comm. – 84 members – org. 2001
Fowlerville – <u>No statistics</u>
Love Mercy Ministries – <u>No statistics</u>
New Covenant – <u>No statistics</u>

Apportionments show 68 active plus 7 New Start churches
List - 75 churches
Net = 73 churches

<u>Summary</u>
1 Inactive
1 Disorganized
7 No statistics (Mission)
1 organized in 2005

*New Start Survivor in 2009

Appendix

Eastern Michigan
Nazarene
2006

Anchor Bay - 107 members – org. 1989
Armada – 52 members – org. 2003
Chelsea – 23 members – org. 1996
Clio Comm. – No statistics – org. 2006
*Crossroads – 55 members – Morning Ill. Re- org. 2002
Detroit New Hope – 49 members – org. 1982
Dundee – 45 mmembers – org. 2002
Everyword Ministries – No statistics – <u>Inactive</u>
Fowlerville – No statistics – org. 2006
Harvest Comm. – 21 members – org. 1943
Living Water – 58 members – org. 1964
Mount Morris – 11 members - org. 1953
Orchard Ridge – 80 members – org. 2005
Deer Park – No statistics – <u>Mission</u>
East Side– No statistics – <u>Mission</u>
Flint New Life – No statistics – <u>Mission</u>
Flushing Comm. – <u>Mission</u> - 90 members – org. 2001
Love Mercy Ministries – <u>Mission</u>-20 members
New Covenant – No Statistics - Mission

Apportionment shows 68 active plus 7 New Start churches
Listed – 75 churches
Net = 74 churches

<u>Summary</u>
7 No statistics
2 Organized this year
6 Mission
1 Inactive

Appendix

Eastern Michigan
Nazarene
2007

Anchor Bay – 107 membership – <u>inactive</u>
*Armada – 58 members– org. 2004
Chelsea – 27 members – org. 1996
Clio – 48 members – org. 2006
Crossroads – 55 members – 58 A.M. attendance – reorg. 2002
Detroit New Hope – 50 members – org. 1983
Dundee – 57 members – org. 2002
Everyword Ministires – <u>inactive</u>
Flushing Comm. – 102 members – org. 2001
Fowlerville – 52 members – org. 2006
Harvest Comm. – 20 members – org. 1943
Living Water – 46 members – 42 A.M. – org. 1965
Mount Morris – 8 members – org. 1954
Orchard Ridge – 171 members - org. 2005
Deer Park – No statistics – <u>Mission</u>
East Side –<u> Mission -</u> <u>dropped</u>
Flint New Life Mission – 5 members
Love Mercy Ministries – 55 members - .A.M. 35 attendance – <u>Mission</u>
New Covenant – No statistics - <u>Mission</u>

Apportionments show 70 active churches plus 4 missions
Listed – 74 churches
Net = 71 churches

<u>Summary</u>
2 No Statistics
2 Inactive
1 Dropped
0 Organized

Apendix

Eastern Michigan
Nazarene
2008

Anchor Bay – 107 members – <u>inactive</u> – org. 1989
Armada – 56 members – org. 2004
Chelsea – 31 members – org. 1996
Clio – 27 members – org. 2006
Crossroads – 59 members - Reorg. 2002 – (61 members 1984)
Dundee – 60 members – org. 2002
Everyword Ministries – <u>inactive</u>
Flushing Comm. – 104 members – org. 2001
Fowlerville – 56 members – org. 2006
Harvest Comm. – 20 members – org. 1943
Living Water – org. 1965
*Mount Morris – 7 members – A.M. attendance 2
New Covenant – Mission – <u>inactive</u> – <u>dropped</u>
Orchard Ridge – 154 members – org. 2005
Deer Park - Mission – Grand Blanc
Flint New life – Mission – org. 2008
Holly – Mission – <u>New Start</u> - 2008
Love Mercy Ministries – 72 members - Mission
New Covenant – <u>inactive</u> – <u>dropped</u>

Apportionments show 69 active plus 4 mission churches
Listed – 73 churches
Net = 69 churches

<u>Summary</u>
2 Inactive
1 New Start
2 Dropped
1 Organized

Appendix
Eastern Michigan
Nazarene
2009

Anchor Bay – <u>inactive</u>
Armada – 56 members – org. 2003
Clio Comm. – 34 members – org. 2006
Corrnerstone – 46 members – org. 1961
Crossroads (was Christ Community) <u>inactive</u> - org. 1980 – shut down 2001 – Restart 2002 - inactive 2009
Crosswalk Comm. – 41 members – org. 1934
Detroit New Hope – 60 members – org. 1982
Dundee Comm. – 74 members – org. 2002
Everyword Ministries – <u>inactive</u> – listed in 2002
Fenton – 130 members – org. 1993
Flint Abundant Grace – 84 members – org. 1990
*Flint New Life – 17 members – org. 2008
Flushing Comm. – 107 members – org. 2001 (listed as church 1972)
Fowlerville – 71 members – org. 2006
Harvest Comm. – 23 members – (after 8 years) org. 1943
Living Water – <u>inactive</u> – org. 1965
Mount Morris – <u>disorganized</u> - 2009
Orchard Ridge – 150 members – org. 2005
Deer Park – <u>dropped</u> - Grand Blanc listed <u>inactive</u> 1973 (36 years ago)
Holly – New Start (restart?) listed 1972 with 20 members (37 years ago)
Love Mercy Ministries – 72 members - Mission

Apportionments – Dropped from the 2009 minutes
Listed 70 churches
Net = 64 churches

<u>Summary</u>
4 Inactive
1 Disorganized
1 Dropped

Appendix
Eastern Michigan Nazarene
2002-2009
Summary
Church Status

Inactive
1. Anchor Bay
2. Everyword Ministries.
3. Living Water
4. Deer Park
5. New Covenant
6. Flat Rock
7. North Oaks

7

Merger
1. Deer Park to Holly
2. Beecher Comm. To Flint First
3. Flint East to Flint New Life

3

Died

Name Change
1. Cornerstone
2. Crossroads
3. Crosswalk
4. Flint New Life

4

New Start
1. Dundee
2. Armada
*. Crossroads (Restart)
3. Clio Comm.
4. Flint New Life
5. Flushing Comm.
6. Lake Comm.
7. Love Mercy
8. New Covenant
9. New Heights
10. Northpointe
11. Orchard Ridge
*Deer Park (in and out for 37 years)
12. East Side
13. Fowlerville
*Holly (in and out for 36 years)

13

2 Restarts
Inactive - Crossroads
Dropped - Deer Park

Disorganized
1. Sterling Heights
2. Flint Westgate
3. North Oaks
4. Lake Comm.
5. New Heights
6. Northpointe
7. Flat Rock
8. Mount Morris
9. New Covenant
10. Everyword Ministries
11. Eastside

11

Organized
1. Crossroads
2. Dundee
3. Armada
4. Orchard Ridge
5. Clio Comm.
6. Fowlerville
7. Flint New Life

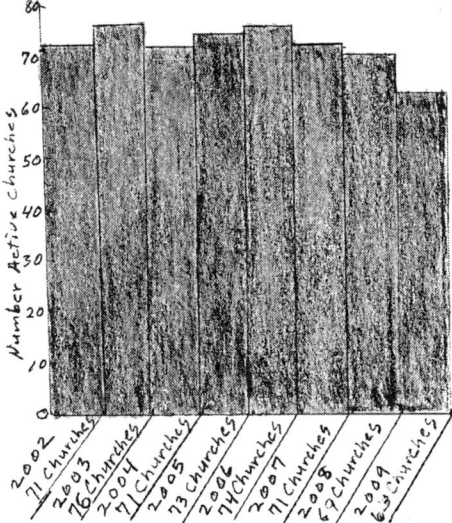

Appendix
Eastern Michigan District Nazarene
Net Active Church List
2002 - 2009

2002 71 Churches
2003 76 Churches
2004 71 Churches
2005 73 Churches
2006 74 Churches
2007 71 Churches
2008 62 Churches
2009 63 Churches

1972 78 Churches

In 2009 Nazarenes had 15 less organized Churches then they did in 1972.

over this period
Disorganized

1. Sterling Heights
2. Flint Westgate
3. North Oaks
4. Lake Comm.
5. New Heights
6. Northpointe
7. Flat Rock
8. Mount Morris
9. New Covenant
10. Every Word
11. Eastside

Mergers —

12. Deer Park to Holly
13. Beecher Comm. to First Church
14. Flint East to Flint New Life

Summary
11 Disorganized
2 Inactive

Topsy Turvy in The Church of the Nazarene

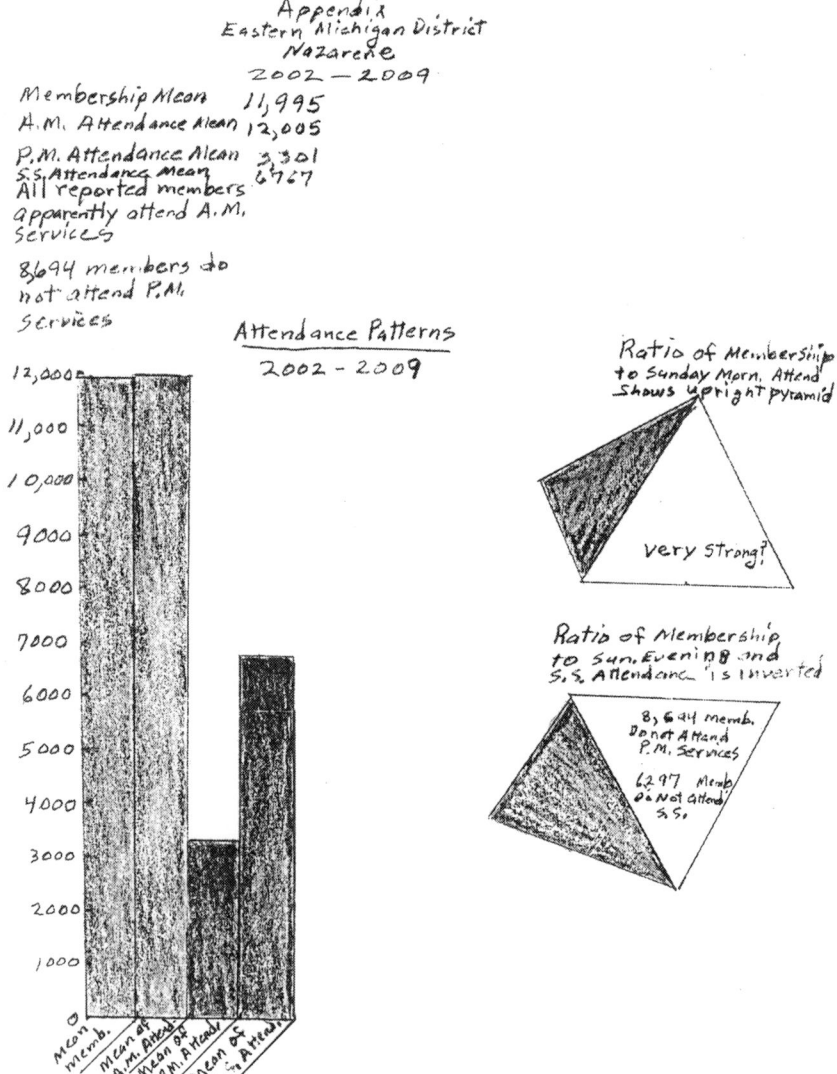

Appendix
Eastern Michigan District
Nazarene
2002 - 2009

Membership Mean 11,995
A.M. Attendance Mean 12,005
P.M. Attendance Mean 3,301
S.S. Attendance Mean 6,767
All reported members apparently attend A.M. services

8,694 members do not attend P.M. services

Attendance Patterns 2002 - 2009

Ratio of Membership to Sunday Morn. Attend. shows upright pyramid

Very Strong!

Ratio of Membership to Sun. Evening and S.S. Attendance is inverted

8,694 memb. Do not Attend P.M. services

6,297 Memb Do not attend S.S.

Topsy Turvy in The Church of the Nazarene

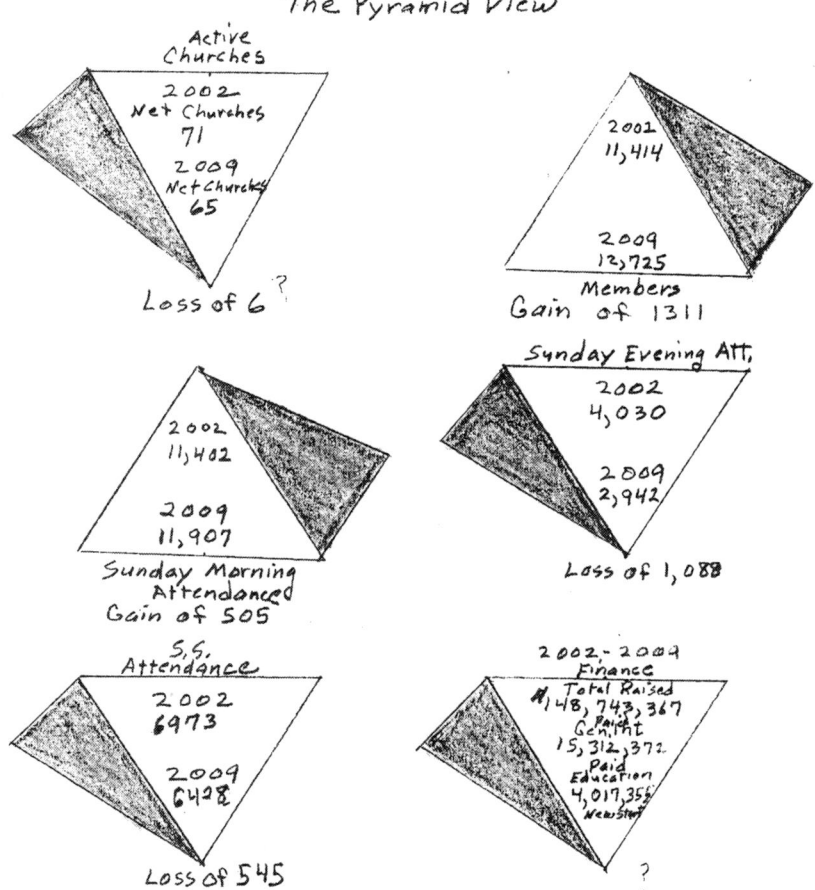

Appendix
Eastern Michigan Nazarene
Examples of Variables in Nazarene Reporting
Three Sources Information -Nazarene Minutes

*1. Home Mission Budget – Not Disbursement
2. Financial Statistical – Home Missions
3. Paid District Interests – Home Missions and New Starts
Col 11A & 11Col.B. Combined

Year	#1	#2	#3
2002	$242,136	$249,615	$210,715
2003	499,756	185,009	275,278
2004	324,418	285,003	282,396
2005	434,610	193,861	252,227
2006	139,000	147,446	29,529
2007	87,000	72,462	31,007
2008	62,500	139,932	17,430
2009	Available on request	100,774	700

*Districts do not report in the same ways. Columns 2 and 3 do not agree even though they reflect disbursements. However, trends are apparent.

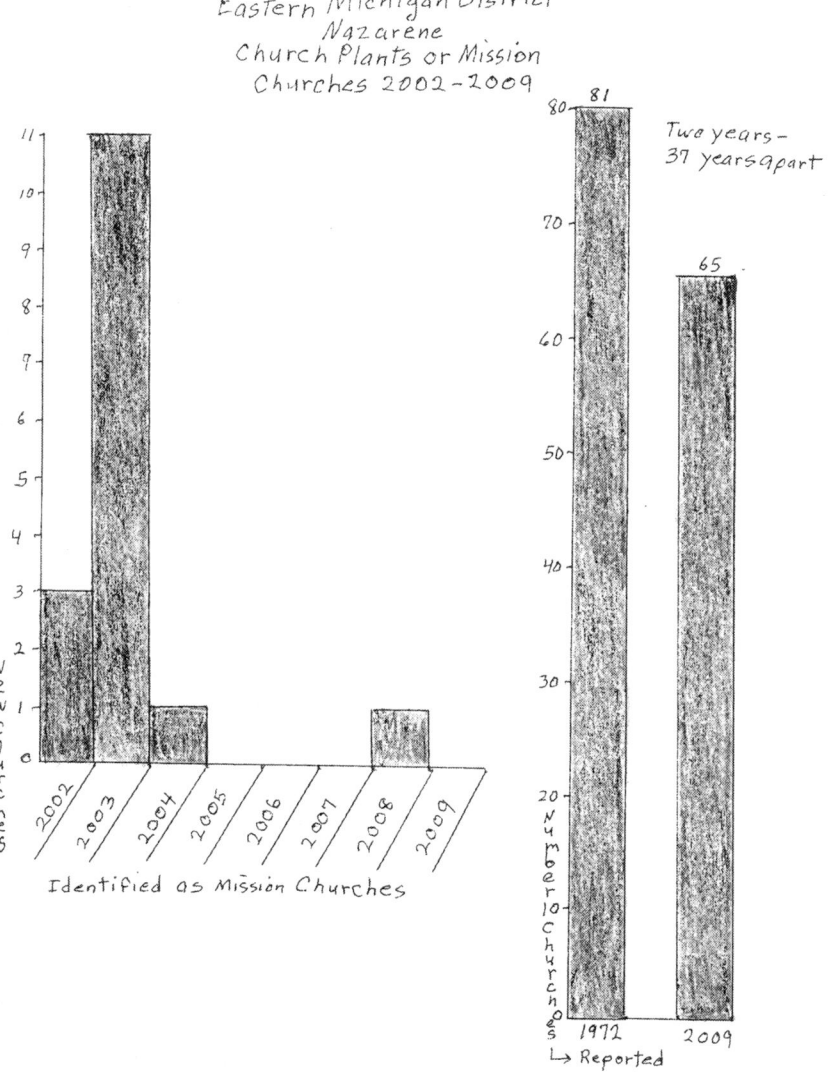

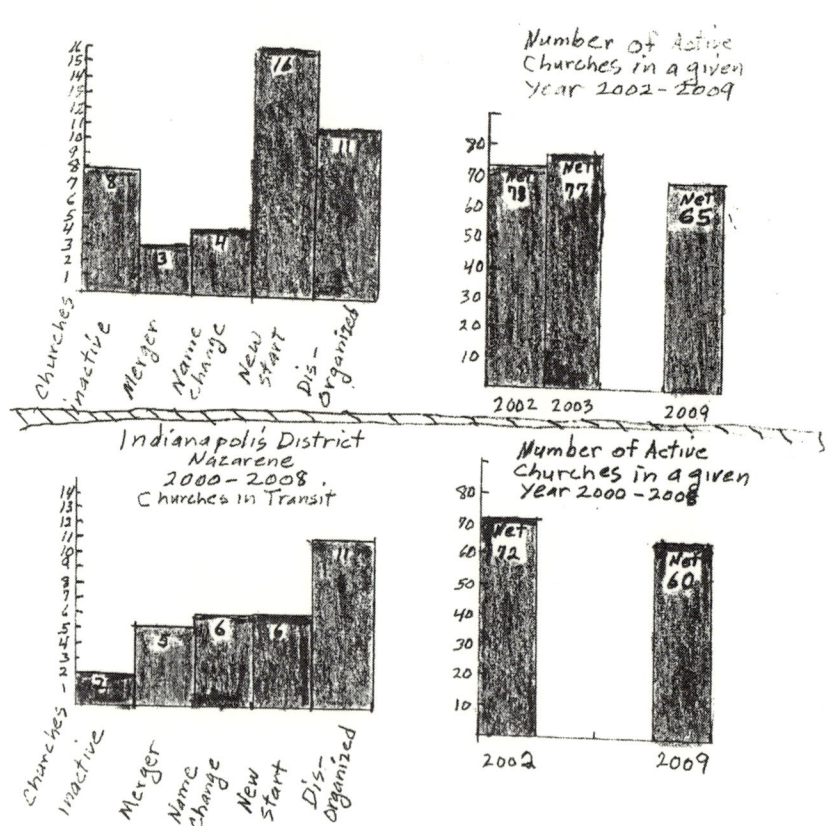

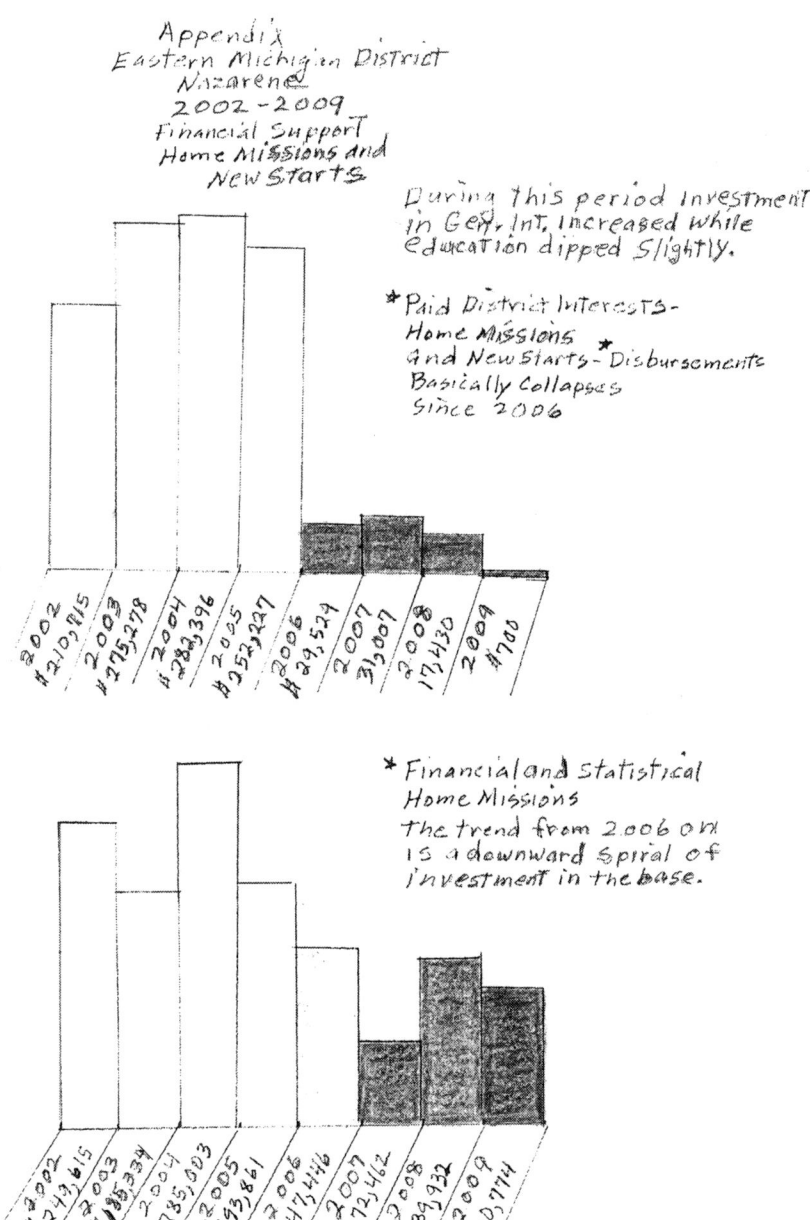

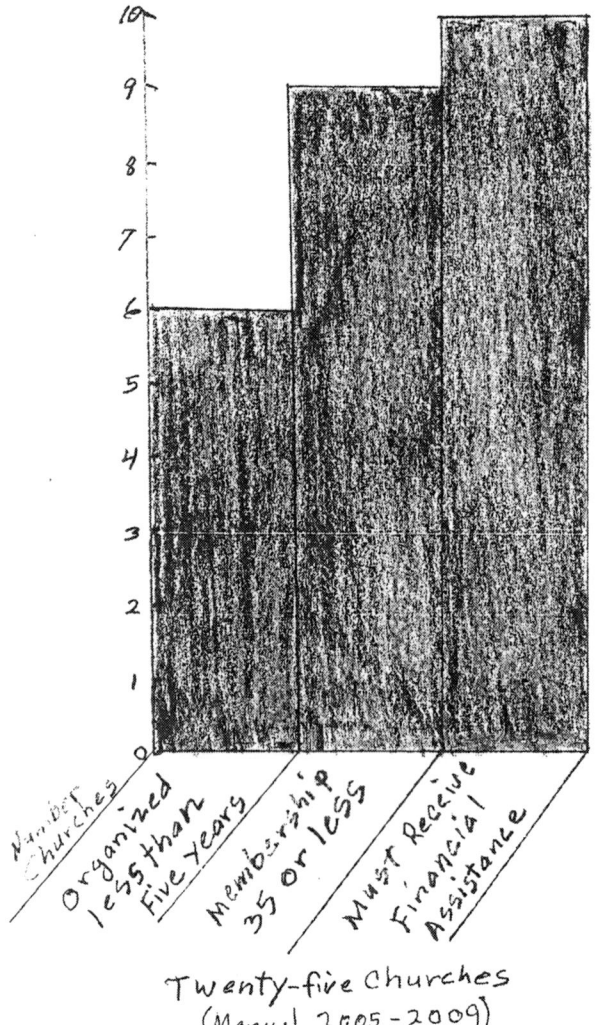

Appendix
Chapter 13
Eastern Michigan District
Pastoral Appointments 2009
Manual Requires One of Following;

I. <u>Organized less than five years.</u>
   1. Orchard Ridge – org. 2005 – 150 members.
   2. Fowlerville – org. 2006 – 71 members.
   3. Clio Community – org. 2006 – 34 members.
   4. Flint New Life – org. 2008 – 17 members
   5. Love Mercy Ministries – CTM – 72 members.
   6. Holly – CTM – Has been in and out for 30 years.

II. <u>Membership 35 or less</u>
   1. Beulah – org. 1914 – 30 members.
   2. Cass City – org. 1924 – 13 members.
   3. Bluewater – org. 1938 – 25 members
   4. Harvest Community – org. 1943 – 23 members.
   5. Ann Arbor First – org. 1944 – 24 members.
   6. Lindenwood – org. 1944 – 12 members.
   7. Bad Axe – org. 1951 – 30 members.
   8. Filian – org. 1955 – 21 members
   9. (Christ Community) Crossroads – Reorg. 2002 – Dead 2009.

III. <u>Must Receive Financial Assistance</u>
   1. Millington – org. 1920 – 57 members.
   2. Crosswalk – org. 1934 – 41 members
   3. Silver Lake – org. 1934 – 117 members
   4. Argentine – org. 1939 – 45 members.
   5. Merritt Road – org. 1940 – 42 members.
   6. Otter Lake – org. 1944 – 53 members.
   7. Imlay City – org. 1955 – 39 members.
   8. Cornerstone – org. 1961 – 46 members.
   9. Flint Abundant Grace – org. 1990 – 84 members.
   10. Dundee – org. 2002 – 74 members.

What does the above mean? It means that 36% of the existing, active churches are in an unhealthy condition. Most of these churches are so weak that their survival is in doubt. It takes a D.S. and an assistant to supervise 45 healthy and 25 unhealthy churches. It costs about one half million to run a district office. The above churches had a combined membership of 1120.

Appendix
Eastern Michigan History

New Plants dead in 2009

2002	Seed Money	
Lake Community	$77,104	dead
Northpointe Community	7,287	dead
North Oaks	14,619	dead
2003		
Northpointe	23,565	dead
Lake Community	4,939	dead
Crossroads	195,000	dead
2004		
Grand Blanc (Deer Park)	11,675	dead
Lake Community	38,271	dead
New Covenant	25,975	dead
New Heights	11,259	dead
Northpointe	13,883	dead

Total $423,577

Spent on churches which died for the above 3 years.

2005
New Church Support not itemized $96,053

The author did not pursue this any further. However, it is a sound bite of what happened to some New Starts and restarts.

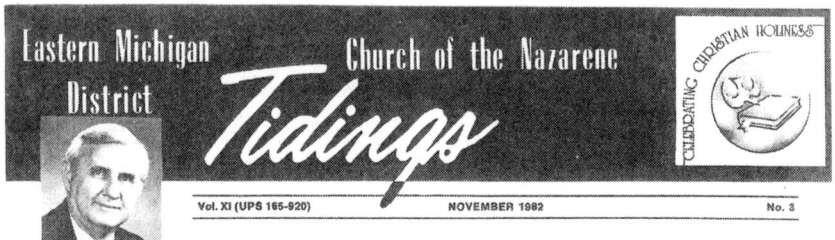

Rev. and Mrs. Steve Floyd Installed at Holly

Shown in the photo with the Floyds are Rev. and Mrs. Eugene Frame. Richfield Church sponsored a revival with their pastor as evangelist and gave $1,000.00 in materials and over 100 man hours of work to the Holly Church.

In 2008, Holly was called a New Start

Appendix
D.S. Exaggerations
Indianapolis District

2004 D.S. Report
 Is it any wonder that there are more Nazarene students on the campus of Olivet than any other Nazarene educational institution."

2004 Nazarene Commissioner of Education statistics indicated that Olivet University was in the 7th place out of the ten Nazarene institutions in the U.S. This is 51% Nazarene students. In 2009, it had a student body of 38% Nazarenes, placing it in 8th position.

2007 Raised 11,594,054 D.S. Report.
Raised 11,413,743 under financial report.
2008 "During the last eight years we have paid our Allocations to others 100%." D.S. Report
2007 "We paid 96.5 percent of our district allocation."
2006 "The district made up the difference so that allocations were paid 100 percent." ". . . We cannot do that in the future."
2005 "As of July 21, we had paid $767,101 of our world Evangelism Fund which is only 97.38 percent of our allocation. This was a major disappointment to me . . . "
2004 Allocations paid 100 percent with help of district.
2003 Fair Share allocation paid 95.92 percent.
2002 Fair Share allocation was 96 percent paid.
2001 Fair Share allocation was 94.5 percent paid.
2000 All allocations paid 100 percent.
2009 Column ten reads 9,070 – D.S. reports 9,197. This is 127 more members than Column ten reports.

Appendix
Eastern Michigan District
D.S. Exaggerations

2,005 D.S. Report on Flushing Averaging over 400. Flushing was active church in 1972, 1984.

2005 M.W. Avg. 346 Memb. 84
2006 M.W. Avg. 423 Memb. 90
2007 M.W. Avg. 453 Memb. 102
2008 M.W. Avg. 424 Memb. 104
2009 M.W. Avg. 245 Memb. 107

Flushing cited as a New Start by D.S. in 2005 report. It was called a mission in 2002. Someone has difficulty delineating a New Start from a Restart. I do not know how long it was a church before 1972. It was at least an active Nazarene Church 33 years ago.

Flushing did not achieve the average cited by the D.S. until 2006. Perhaps his report was anticipatory.

Since 2007. Flushing has had a decline of nearly 50% in Morning Worship attendance.

2005 D.S. Report on Orchard Ridge averaging 250 a week.

M.W. 122
M.W. 190 Memb. 80
M.W. 225 Memb. 171
M.W. 219 Memb. 154
M.W. 203 Memb. 150

Orchard Ridge has yet to achieve an average of 250 a week which was cited in the 2005 D.S. Report. Its membership is down from 2007. Morning worship attendance is also down from 2007.

Appendix
Eastern Michigan District
Nazarene
Attendance & Finance

Attendance

Year	Col. 10 Membership	A.M. Attendance	P.M. Attendance	Comb. Adult-Child Sunday School
2002	11,414	11,402	4,030	6,973
2003	11,369	11,506	3,554	6,742
2004	11,681	11,917	3,467	6,919
2005	11,794	11,945	3,558	6,836
2006	11,990	12,464	3,202	6,548
2007	12,450	12,731	2,565	7.061
2008	12,538	12,168	3,088	6,632
2009	12,725	11,907	2,942	6,428
Gain 8 years	Gain 1311	Gain 505 - over 100% attendance compared to members?	Loss 1,088 - 28% of members attend P.M. services	Loss 545 - 51% of members attend S.S.

Mean membership is 11,995
Mean of A.M. attendance 12,005
Mean of P.M. attendance 3301
Mean of Sunday School attendance 6767
Attendance Patterns: 100% of Membership attend Sunday Morning?
                        28% of Membership attend Sunday Evening.

2002-2009 Financial

	Raised All Purposes	Paid General Interests	Paid Colleges	Comb. Col. 11A, 11B. Paid Home Mission/ New Start
2002	17,416,348	1,886,158	510,129	210,715
2003	17,810,231	1,993,088	527,049	275,278
2004	19,183,482	2,009,672	526,983	282,396
2005	14,921,166	1,539,661	416,827	252,227
2006	19,169,339	2,206,214	549,614	91,412
2007	20,264,408	1,954,928	515,486	102,968
2008	21,152,353	1,959,185	527,565	157,362
2009	18,826,040	1,763,466	443,702	101,474
Totals	$148,743,367	$15,312,372	$4,017,355	$1,473,832

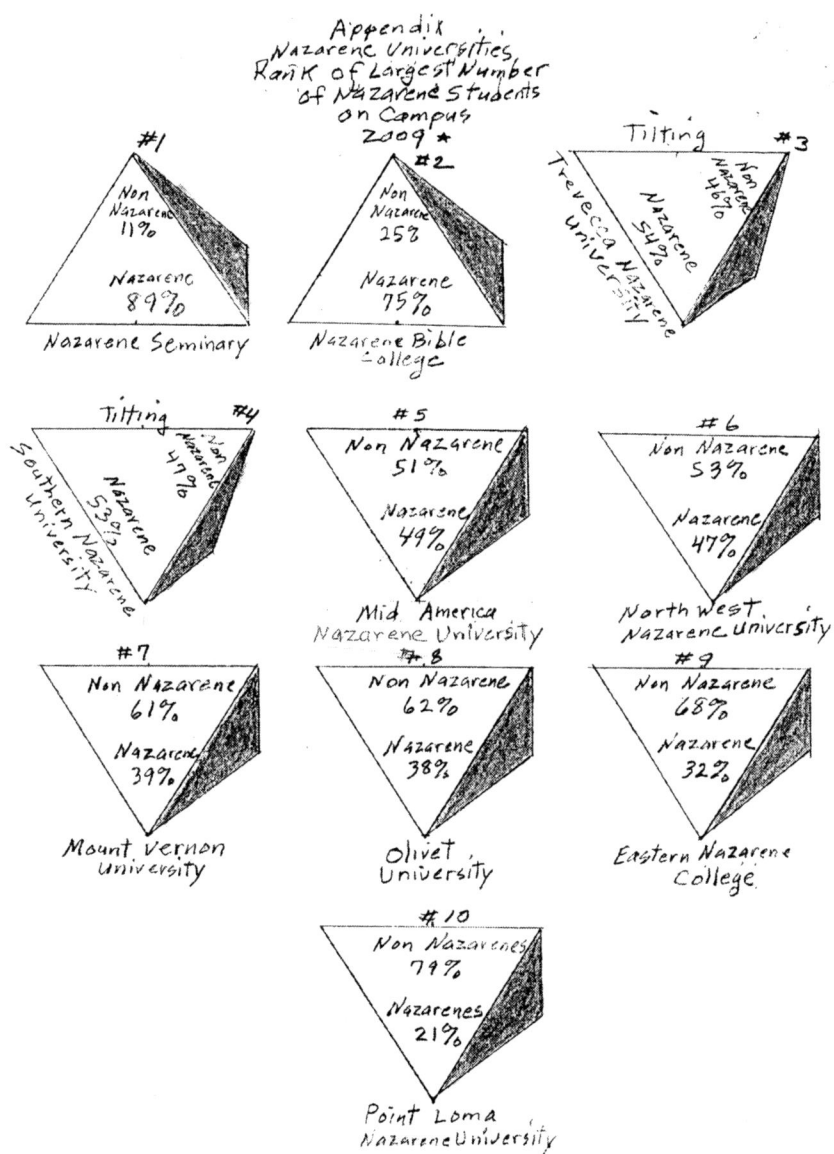

Appendix
Nazarene Universities
And Graduate Schools
2004 and 2009 U.S.

Rank of numbers of Nazarene students in undergraduate programs. Seminary – rank of number of Nazarene students in graduate program.

College	2004 Rank Nazarene.	Non-Nazarene	College	2009 Rank Nazarene.	Non-Nazarene.	Gain/Loss
1 Seminary	88%	12%	1 Seminary	89%	11%	Gain - 1%
2 Bible College	85%	15%	2 Bible College	75%	25%	Loss - 10%
3 Southern U.	64%	36%	3 Trevecca U.	54%	46%	Loss - 10%
4 Trevecca U.	61%	39%	4 Southern U.	53%	47%	Loss – 11%
5 Mid–America U.	58%	42%	5 Mid-America U.	49%	51%	Loss – 9%
6 Northwest U.	57%	43%	6. Northwest U.	47%	53%	Loss – 10%
*7 Olivet U.	51%	49%	7 Mt. Vernon U.	39%	61%	Loss – 9%
8. Mt. Vernon U.	48%	52%	*8 Olivet U.	38%	62%	Loss – 13%
9 Eastern College.	39%	61%	9 Eastern College.	32%	68%	Loss – 7%
10. Point Loma U.	26%	74%	1. Point Loma U.	21%	79%	Loss – 5%

Endnotes

Chapter One
1. Girven, E.A., <u>Phineas F Bresee: A Prince in Israel</u>, (Nazarene Publishing House, 1916).
2. Qualben, L.P., <u>A History of The Christian Church</u>, (Nelson & Sons, N.Y., 1933).
3. Ibid.
4. Ibid.
5. Girven, E.A., <u>Phineas F. Bresee: A Prince in Israel</u>, (Nazarene Publishing House, 1916).

Chapter Two
6. Coleridge, Samuel, <u>The Rhyme of the Ancient Mariner</u>.

Chapter Five
7. Coulter, F.R., <u>The Holy Bible In Its Original Order</u>, (York Publishing Co., 2007).
8. Robinson, Robert, <u>Come Thou Fount of Every Blessing</u>, (Public Domain, 1790), 2nd Stanza.

Chapter Six
9. Coulter, F.R., <u>The Holy Bible In Its Original Order</u>, (York Publishing Co., 2007).

Chapter Ten
10. Thompson, N.H., <u>The Prince</u>, by Niccolo Machiavelli, (Public Domain, Oxford at the Clarendon Press, London: Humphrey Milford, 1913), P. 63.
11. Ibid., P. 63.
12. Coulter, F.R., <u>The Holy Bible In Its Original Order</u>, (York Publishing Co., 2007).
13. Ibid.

14. Ibid.
15. Ibid.
16. Coleridge, Samuel, Rhyme of the Ancient Mariner.
17. Coulter, F.R., The Holy Bible In Its Original Order, (York Publishing Co., 2007).
18. Ibid.
19. Ibid.
20. Ibid.
21. Thompson, N.H., The Prince, by Niccolo Machiavelli, (Public Domain, Oxford at the Clarendon Press, London: Humphrey Milford, 1913), PP. 9, 10.
22 Ibid., P. 72.
23. Ibid., P. 110.
24. Ibid., PP. 118,119.
25. Ibid., P. 120.
26. Ibid., P. 126.
27. Ibid., P. 126.
28. Ibid., P. 127.
29. Ibid., P. 129.
30. The Lost Books of the Bible, (Peabody Museum of American Archaeology and Ethnology, Cambridge, 1901), P. 213.
31. Coulter, R.R., The Holy Bible In Its Original Order, (York Publishing Co., 2007).
32. Ibid.
33. Miles, Austin, Don't Call Me Brother, Prometheus Books, 1989.

Chapter Eleven
34. Indianapolis District Minutes, (Nazarene, 2008), P. 86.
35. Eastern Michigan District Minutes, (Nazarene, 2009), P. 68, 69.
36. Indianapolis District Minutes, (Nazarene, 2007), P. 86.
37. Eastern Michigan District Minutes, (Nazarene, 2008), PP. 73, 74.
38. Indianapolis District Minutes, (Nazarene, 2006), P. 83.
39. Eastern Michigan District Minutes, (Nazarene, 2007), PP. 79, 80.
40. Indianapolis District Minutes, (Nazarene, 2005), P. 80.
41. Eastern Michigan District Minutes, (Nazarene, 2006), P. 80.
42. Indianapolis District Minutes, (Nazarene, 2004), P. 85.

43. Eastern Michigan District Minutes, (Nazarene, 2005), P. 76.
44. Indianapolis District Minutes, (Nazarene, 2003), P. 82.
45. Eastern Michigan District Minutes, (Nazarene, 2004), P. 82.
46. Indianapolis District Minutes, (Nazarene, 2000-2007), D.S. Reports
47. Eastern Michigan District Minutes, (Nazarene, 2002-2009), D.S. Reports
48. First Church Indianapolis, (Nazarene, District Minutes, 2005), P. 96.
49. Coulter, F.R. The Holy Bible In Its Original Order, (York Publishing Co., 2007).
50. Indianapolis District Minutes, (Nazarene, 2003), P. 57.

Chapter Twelve
51. Coulter, F. R., The Holy Bible In Its Original Order, (York Publishing Co., 2007).
52. Ibid.

Chapter Thirteen
53. Indianapolis District Minutes, (Nazarene, 2000-2008), D.S. Reports.
54. Manual, (2005-2008), Church of the Nazarene, (Nazarene Publishing House), Par.116.
55. Holiness Today, July-Aug., 2009, P. 8 (By Permission).
56. Holiness Today, July-Aug., 2009, P. 8 (By Permission).
57. Holiness Today, July–Aug. 2009, P. 39 (By Permission).
58. Holiness Today, Nov.-Dec., 2008, P. 30 (By Permission).
59. Ibid. P. 30 (By Permission).
60. Holiness Today, July-Aug., 2009, P. 8 (By Permission).
61. Holiness Today, Nov-Dec., 2009, P. 30 (By Permission).
62. Holiness Today, Sept.-Oct., 2009, P. 30 (By Permission).
63. Holiness Today, July-Aug., 2009, P. 17 (By Permission).
64. Holiness Today, July-Aug., 2009, P. 37 (By Permission).
65. Quanstrom, Mark, A Century of Holiness Theology, (Beacon Hill Press, 2004). PP. 137-169.
66. Ibid.

Chapter Fourteen
67. Coulter, F.R., The Holy Bible in Its Original Order, (York Publishing Company).

68. Leslie, Emma, Peter the Apprentice, (The Religious Tract Society – London, 1873). P.113.
69. Miles, Austin, Don't Call Me Brother, (Prometheus Books, 1989). PP. 315, 316.
70. Hogue, W.T., Introduction to: History of the Free Methodist Church. (The Free Methodist Publishing House, 1915). P. 10.
71. Coulter, F.R., The Holy Bible in Its Original Order, (York Publishing Co., 2007).
72. Ibid.
73. Wesley, Charles; Elvey, George J. Soldiers of Christ Arise. (Public Domain, Second Stanza, 1749.

Breinigsville, PA USA
05 January 2011
R4021500001B/R40215PG252663BVX1B/1/P